Seeing the Elephant

Seeing the Elephant

by
Harold Lawrence

This book is printed on acid-free paper which conforms to the American National Standard Z39.48-1984 Permanence of Paper for Printed Library Materials. Paper that conforms to this standard's requirements for pH, alkaline reserve and freedom from groundwood is anticipated to last several hundred years without significant deterioration under normal library use and storage conditions.

ISBN: 1-890307-28-9

Copyright © 1999

Cover courtesy Zoo Atlanta
and
Family Photographs

Boyd Publishing Company
PO Box 367
Milledgeville, GA 31061

Also by Harold Lawrence

Southland
Memory Hill
Voice of the Turtle

To Mac
Who always looked for it

Acknowledgements

Many of the poems written here and in other volumes reflect the stories and suggestions of numerous people. I have often asked them, "How would you end this story?" and received good insight from those willing to lend a particular viewpoint on a subject or a tale that could take more than one direction. It is impossible to list all who have made such contributions, and I will not attempt it.

Those who have volunteered ideas for many of the stories in this volume are named with the titles: "Hired Help" Louis Veatch, "Better Off Dead" Charles Henson, "Death Knell" Ed Nelson, "Bloody Buckets" William Meeler, "Holy Ground"& "Pissin'Rock" Gary Swinger, "Living to Tell It" James Dorsey, "Traders" Jim Mills, "No Man's Land" Ryan Seawright, "Slaying the Dragon" Mac McConnell (my father-in-law), "Herman's Thumb" Joyce Stiefel, "Pallet Babies" Horace Norman, "Making Sure" Virgil Lawrence (my grand-father), "West Hell" Franklin Council, "Midnight Grill" the result of a dinner table conversation with my children.

Other pieces reflect the influence of these and others. I am indebted to Beaufort Cranford and William Mallard for editing, to Ruth Cranford, Linda Lawrence and James Dorsey for proofreading, to Brenda Phillips for formating and layout of the text, and to all who have taken an interest and given an ear to the themes and threads running through these stories.

Introduction

In his latest collection of poems Harold Lawrence, who has fascinated us with three previous volumes, "sees the elephant," that is, he probes for moments that pierce the ordinary and the routine to astound us with how things really are. The disclosure leaves us never the same. In probably the finest poem in the collection, "Silver Bullet" (p. 109), a farmer waits up nights for a killer cat that has despoiled him, one by one, of all his stock of animals. The beast kills, not for hunger or even for territory, but as "a presence stalking the world / with its black heart fixed on him / . . . singular in its unerring will." His ultimate meeting with the cat is almost an at-homeness "with its malevolence," a commingling. He realizes the webbed complexity of himself, the beast, the world, good and evil. The event changes him forever.

In most of the collection the shapes of death and loss constitute "the elephant." Human demise strikes hard. Yet we miss the fruitfulness of the book if we miss the kindliness of the unveiled "beyond." The "elephant" is a bestial introduction to the soul's true hope, as in "Behind the Door" (p.209);

> . . . to us is given
> the crispness of this moment
> and the silks of peaceful nights
> while all else the heart requires
> lies just behind the door.

Or the voice of the poet finally wishes for us

> that as you look in the eyes of age
> you may behold the eyes of a child
> and that the last day like the first
> will be fresh with wonder.   "Postscript" (p. 214)

The setting for the poems, as with so many of Lawrence's previous pieces is the forested lands, farmlands, and small towns of Middle Georgia that he knows so well. We see "the sun bleeding like a sieve" (p. 65), "fireflies, wings tucked in prayer" (p.122), or the armadillo, "a bold, pint-sized conquistador" (p. 91). We know the "inner gyroscopes of birds" (p.139), the single crow flying "like a mote in the mind's eye" (p.142), and cicadas "telegraphing joy among themselves" (p.167). We remember "those old smiling farms / that grinned like waving grandparents / from the banks of unpaved county roads" (p.33). And we get the comic horse-laugh of someone "with that got-caught look of a dog / trying to pass persimmon seeds" (p.171).

We decline and shrivel with human life that the years discard. "The best of times slip gently from the bough" (p.128).

> All the iron men have rusted
> their women worn down like shovels
> and their time like the rubble heaps
> of old chimneyed houseplaces   "Reminders" (p.125)

Lawrence tells in "Marasmus" (p. 159) of an aging farmwife whose husband lies frail and dying, who nevertheless, on Sunday afternoon, leaves him abed and goes out to the garage to sit quietly in the old car that used to take them for a Sunday ride. Or a young war-widow, withdrawing from reality, gathers fodder in the field, a daydream place for her,

> free from the intrusions of the house
> and the old ones on their bedpans
> calling out to redefine her world . . .

Nor does she

> join widows old and round
> who scratch about in cemetery plots

but slips mentally back into girlhood, loose from the reality of empty, withered cornstalks ("Sanctuary" p. 11).

For all such people caught in bleakness, Lawrence narrates no relief. Yet his poems dignify the wasted figures. About Willy Loman in *Death of a Salesman* his wife Linda says: ". . . he's a human being, and a terrible thing is happening to him. So attention must be paid." Poems pay attention. Lawrence's "seeing the elephant" is like Martin Heidegger's "eruption of being," or like the terrible moment when Oedipus learns from the shepherd the secret of his origins. And Lawrence's poetry includes a crucial element: the compassion that will not surrender human dignity everywhere around us, even in the elephant's worst grip.

William Mallard
Emory University
Atlanta, Georgia

How many times and in how many ways does one see the elephant? It is sensed and sighted in the owning of bizarre yet reconstituting experiences. War, death, hardship, privation and conversion are all occasions to live through to the other side and, from that advantage, to have "seen the elephant." This was a catch phrase for those going West in the 1830s and 1840s and for those who fought in the War Between the States and in the subsequent Indian wars of the West. It has also been used to describe the coincidental, the accidental and the serendipitous. "Seeing the elephant" describes a state of being for those who have coped with outer threat and inner darkness, who have been shaped by unnatural events and who have salvaged the experiences and distilled their defining moments like one who wrings the proper vintage from a yield of grapes.

Table of Contents

Under the Toadstool   1

Charmer   2

The Shining Path   4

Old Soldier   6

Resurrection   8

Sanctuary   11

Deep-Sixed   13

Across the Dead Line   15

Coca-Cola Crate Conversations   16

Old Tales   19

Seeing the Elephant   20

Stomping Ground   24

Cat Heads   25

Hired Help   27

Slaying the Dragon   28

Traders   30

Beekeepers   31

A Dirge of the Land   33

Living to Tell It	34
Immigrants	36
Leviathan	37
Old Man Mose	39
Snow in the South	41
Far Fields	44
Death Knell	45
Stations in Hell	48
Touch of Frost	50
Stone Soup	52
Eighth Sister	53
Through the Needle's Eye	55
Yard Sale	57
Freak Show	58
Making Sure	59
Leper Colony	61
Cargo	63
At the Candelite Motel	65
Learned in Rain	68

Reflections on Snow Hill   69

Dark Thirty   71

Dear and Wishful Heart   73

My Aunt Jett   74

A Fork Chronicle   82

To Listening Aliens   84

Windmill Hill   85

Holy Ground   86

Chinaberry Wars   88

In the Line of Duty   89

Armadillos   91

Pissin' Rock   92

Broken Covey   95

Iris   96

When Cotton was King   97

Terrapin Shell   99

Honest Flaw   101

More Crate Talk   102

Bereft   105

Gypsy's Curse 106

Sinking Spell 108

Silver Bullet 109

Imposition 114

West Hell 115

Keiser's Pigeons 118

In the Eye of Peril 119

No Man's Land 121

Mowing Fields 122

Midnight Grill 123

Reminders 125

Bedpan Commando 126

Haunts 128

Ambience 129

Consolation 131

Witch's Tit 133

Options 135

Clisbys 136

Just Dead Reckoning 139

Christmas Visit   140

Gray Days   142

Old Friend   143

Polliwogs   144

Homebound   146

Pallet Babies   150

Mehetabel at High Tea   151

Sentinel   153

Kathleen   154

Twelfth Birthday   155

Requiem   156

Hoochie Mama   158

Marasmas   159

Beggared Questions   160

Trailer Trash   161

The First Precept   164

Fishing on the Bottom   165

Cicadas   167

Shades of Pandora   168

Bless Its Little Heart   170

Better Off Dead   171

Magi   173

Bloody Buckets   174

Pretenders   176

Good to Go   177

In Remembrance   179

Techniques   180

Counting Coup   182

Whiling Time   184

Leave a Message   185

Days of Brass   187

Safe Haven   188

Over the Wall   190

A Death in the Woods   191

Signature   192

Fit to Kill   193

Night Beat   195

Crop Duster   196

A Brief Noel   197

At the Submarine Museum   198

Best Way   200

Grave Matters   201

Fire   203

Walking Death   204

Herman's Thumb   206

Homemade Sin   207

Behind the Door   209

End of the Line   210

In Essence   212

Postscript   214

Like the Buddha's famous story
of the divining blind men
we feel the parts and pieces
and think we know the whole
when the fuller revelation
stomps and stamps and trumps
its passion from within us.

Under the Toadstool

Who will sit with me
and watch the dew come up?
Who will wait with me
and look and listen?
Against these pillowed ribs
we can while the time
and enjoy the simple musk
or soak up the brief joys
of light and shade
or behold the pinched faces
of ivory sages in the clouds
furled in their windy robes
and blowing by like ships
as we peek up at them
squinting like sun-kissed cherubs
from under the reddened nutmeg top
from places near and wee.

Who will join me
in this feast of little pleasures?
Who will dine with me
on the wafer and the comb
of sweet content?
Under this pungent stalk
there is room enough to rest
the heads of lesser gods
than those who keep us
vexed with strife and fear
but they would teach us
the songs that play
in the hearts of all warm things
so that we would find the grace
to pause among them
and hear an ecstasy
that is like no other.

Charmer

He cut only the wild cherry
which was death to a cow
and placed the green chips
in a foot tub on the porch
to soak for three full days
and swell to twice their size.

Then he'd lift out the meat
sparkling in the saltbox
and rinse away the brine
and lug it to the smokehouse
where a small fire hissed
and licked the sandy pit.

Each cold-cured piece
gored on sharp hooks
was hung aloft to drip
by sausage dried in sacks
as swollen chips were fed
to raise a thickening smoke.

With a backdrop of odors
aromatic and irresistible
and a footstool pulpit
to hold his tobacco box
he'd squat down and talk
for the next five days.

Children drawn like flies
would stop and light close by
grinning through snaggled teeth
as the seeds of mystic lands
of treasures, wars and kings
were planted safely in them.

The years would root them,
weed them, prune them
so they could spring from flesh
long after the house burned
and the smokehouse fell
and the yard stood empty.

The Shining Path

So clear and visible as she stood there
posing for the photograph that caught it
before two oceans went to war
it stretched smooth and sheer and silvery
illumined by bright prisms long engendered
in the quickening pulse of youth.
As she looked down the long stretch of it
in the split-second opening of the lens
she never guessed her fledgling generation
would be propelled by it so soon
out to its needle-sharp vanishing point
and down the sickening chute of colliding years
or dreamed of being a great-grandmother
ripe and puffed and out of breath
sorting out so many little names
and she could not know how many
of the faces she immortalized and loved
would beckon from across the dead line
or that the salt spray of the Pacific
would etch itself into her knowledge lines
and temper the boundless energies of joy
with endless inner monologues of sorrow
reciting themselves for one deep-sixed
and rocked in the ocean's cradle.

What gleamed before her like a glass bridge
that day she smiled and stepped off
on a sparkling crystal end of it
like a wistful Dorothy wearing magic shoes

cracked and broke in great waxed slabs
on December seventh, nineteen forty-one
at a point far and cold and ice-blue
where time had flared and stamped
with the rampage of an elephant
dangling her doll-like and suspended
on edges jagged and precipitous
above the customary reach of God
where she learned and she remembered
half-hearing while a little girl
old sayings which casually floated by
released like seeds from the pods of those
who lived around her as she played
and griefs that rose and ebbed unnoticed
like distant waves heard in old shells
all building now to a rhythm in her blood
and roaring their Niagaras in her veins
charging her to turn and stumble back
through the last, large, discarded pieces
to take her rightful place among them.

Old Soldier

He sat on the front porch for years
married to the same worn-down spot
that caught the lifting breeze
and never made him hunt for shade
his left sleeve empty and pinned back
like a bird with its wing broken
as he fumbled through coat pockets
worrying with a piece of withered fruit.
Still quite the sage at ninety-four
he struck a typical bearded profile
for the many goings to and from
available for nods and pleasantries
yet poised to spit over the rail
barking grave commands to children
who idled too close to his chair
and doling out advice in large helpings
to any who would pause and profit.
At mealtime he reminded everyone,
"A willful waste makes a woeful want!"
When someone complained about another
he always recited the admonition,
"Mind your own hogs and hominy!"
The little girl skipping to the mailbox
received a daily dose of scorn with,
"Be sure your sins will find you out!"
And when they took him kicking
from the porch to a hospital ward
where he lay restrained and gurgling
giving up his ghost before sundown
his last pronouncement to them was,

"A man's home is his castle!'
spoken while waging a last assault
with the blunt head of a walking cane
to equal one he'd made at Seven Pines
before any of them were born.
They left his chair there in remembrance
until the seat split from the weather
then put it above the barn's rafters
to reside among other family relics
but his sayings were carried with them
and were used from time to time
as ballast for their conversations
and linkage to his life and breath.

Resurrection

He found them over Christmas holidays
while inspecting the spine and ribs
of an ice-glazed shed near death
and graying behind the robust house
lopsided from the calloused brunt
of brittle winds and rain-soaked winters.
They lay flat on the twisted rafters
atop two dressed boards of heart pine
ripped when they built the place
and stored for wistful antebellum uses
that perished with the Confederacy.
He scooped out in double-handfuls
the generations of dried bird droppings
and crumbling bits of gilt and veneer
decorating the aged, ornate frames
before gently lowering them down.
As he lifted the thin wood backing
and pried out the mellowed portraits
billowing frost with every breath
four felt-soft but solemn faces
estranged for more than a century
caught their first glimpse of sunlight
and sent a shiver through his bones
charging him with faint affinities
for hardened chins and oval eyes.

He took them to a shadowed bedroom
where the old one lay under covers
and switched on the bedside lamp
and held the faces right up close.
A bony finger came from warmth

to trace around the spotted images
as a cracked voice floated up
through drowning tides of yellow phlegm
to say to him, "These are your people."
In that next uncomfortable half-hour
while the long silences reminded him
of an audience with an ailing god
pronouncements came in labored breaths
which galvanized their lives with his.
"Those first two came as immigrants
thin as rails from the potato famine. . .
came with just the clothes on their backs
but they knew how to work the fields
and that's how we got this place.
The others are a different line. . .
settled a place called Windmill Hill
but I never knew any more about it.
You got their looks as I see . . .
Now take them out from here. . .
they're all long dead and buried.

That night he lay in frozen dark
while gas logs hissed their warmth
and windows bled from the panes
watching an orange moon chin itself
up and then over the bottom sash
and listening to the faint disturbances
resounding through old clapboards.
The portraits lay in state that night
like a casket resting in the icy hall
and he got up more than once
to check their impassive countenances
in the gray of his moonlit room
and feel their penetrating stares

from orbs set with dull obsidian
appraise him for what he was.
They spoke to him where he stood
with toes stuck to the cold floor
and his heart caught each inflection
as it echoed in the empty vaults.
"Do you not know us? Do you
not long for some word of us?
It was from dust and much spittle
that you were surely made by us.
Part of it has been for nothing
if you do not seek to know."

Sanctuary

The sky may yet rain its lead
on the rows of spent cornstalks
as their drying ribs chafe each other
and the scarecrow in the middle
cocks its head and twists in the wind
with the frozen grin of a straw effigy
presiding over primitive burial places.

She has come to pull the fodder
tying blades together into hands
and balancing them on the tops of stalks
enough to cure and take in bundles
for storage in the barn's dry loft
once the evening damps come up
and the fodder will not shatter.

It looks to be a somber welcoming
with everything a-hush and on the wane
provided the heavy clouds hold back
and grant a soft and solitary afternoon
free from the intrusions of the house
and the old ones on their bedpans
calling out to redefine her world.

Out here near rabbit pills and nettle
hands burning from each tiny razor cut
or stinging from a packsaddle's brush
she is at home in what moves her
back to the imagined safety of a girl
and away from the clutches of one

who will never be back from the war.
She does not grieve as others do
or join widows old and round
who scratch about in cemetery plots
marking their lifeless territories
but stands in these yielding rows
recalling the time she first heard tales
of how a prince would come.

Deep-Sixed

If you could go into the dark recesses
just shy of the forty-fifth parallel
down to the bottom of the deep
where the *Wahoo* sighs and rests
barnacled now and corroded
after fifty years on the bottom
you would know what it is like
to hear the last chiming of the bells
and feel the shock of breath erupt
and drink the rushing stinging brine
on that final fatal plunge
straight to Davey Jones's locker.

Nestled in a bed of sand and silt
the undercurrents touch her softly
when something in her pops and stirs
then gently lull her back to sleep
but bubbles by the thousands
leaked from her fractured hull
in those first silver-boiling hours
seeping from the pressurized gaskets
and breaking the oil-streaked surface
like escaping souls bereft of hope
and pointing toward the unmarked grave
of a steel maiden with her back broken.

Fish play along the ruins of her con
circling wide like that errant torpedo
launched straight and smooth and true
in a tight spread of three

hot and running from the stern tubes
then coming back to haunt and cripple
seconds before their final kill
and spell disaster for the ship and crew
with nothing but a faulted rudder rod. . .
coming back like an unexpected Jonah
to freeze each face in time
and seal the fate of other ships.

There was no time to refit or repair
or ward off the hounding planes
that sent her cracked and bleeding
into the solace of the depths.
With her died all aid to *Tang* and *Tullibee*
whose Mark 18's came back to sting them
just like hers and send them down
but not before that instant recognition
screaming from the nerve endings
in those last long desperate moments
telegraphed from face to frozen face
the mirror image of their greatest foe.

Deep-Sixed: The Wahoo was one of 52 submarines lost in WWII. Thought to have been damaged from the circular return of its own Mark 18 torpedo, it was sunk by the Japanese on 10-11-1943 before it could return to report this phenomenon. Due to its failure to make this report, two other U.S. submarines, *Tang* and *Tullibee*, sank themselves in the firing of their Mark 18's. See: O'Kane, Richard H. *Wahoo.* Bantam Books, 1989, pp. 316-327; O'Kane, Richard H. *Clear the Bridge.* Bantam Books, 1981, pp. 444-455.

Across the Dead Line

Across the dead line
are the soldiers who have died in wars
and the women lost to childbirth
and old ones who simply fell asleep.
They would speak their wisdom to us
and tell us all the words of this life
if they could reach across the gulf
that yawns between our hearts and theirs
but each time their power is flung
like sharp pronged grappling hooks
to gain a biting hold upon us
we shrink back or flinch from fear
and let the larger moment pass
never looking just beyond the curve
that bends the light of all we know
to let us see where we are bound
as we inch toward the last divider.

Coca-Cola Crate Conversations

Outside the door at Webb's filling station
sitting there and shaving off a piece
from a fresh plug of Day's Work
then passing around the open knife
the talk turned to the terrible shape
the world was in and how it seemed
the best had gone from bad to worse
and aimed to bust hell wide open
and wouldn't it be more than something
if a way could be found to take
the sin and meanness out of people.

Then Ed said,
"There was a colored woman I knew
cooked meals at the old Bellflower
before it burned to the ground
you remember where it was
sat right across from the depot . . .
she had a daughter living at home
who used to save old movie magazines
and spend her time cutting out pictures
of all the idols and glamor queens
and every time a new show came out
and one of them would die on screen
or if they'd be named in some scandal
(you know how them people live)
she'd go and find their picture
and set fire to it and bury the ashes
chanting to herself and mumbling
how God didn't need her matches
if He was of a mind to start a fire
but she sure used plenty of them. . .
claimed it would burn out the sin.
People believed she could conjure
until she burned up her mama's house
burned her and her mama up in it

You could see them through the smoke
running around with their hair on fire."

Then Spec said,
"I don't know nothing about that
but back when my daddy was a boy
when they put a body in the ground
a man dressed in black clothes
would come walking out of the woods
after all the people had gone home
and he'd sit down by the fresh grave
and spread a cloth beside it
then eat himself a plate of food
while he closed his eyes and prayed
for God to let him take away the sin
like he was eating it and swallering it.
Everybody back there called him preacher
but he weren't no more one than you. . .
That went on until I was born
and they had this burial at Damascus
where somebody hid out to watch him
but he never showed up for it
or came to one after that.
Guess he must have left out or died . . .
Makes me wonder who buried him."

Then Bob said,
"You talking about forgiving sin
what became of that German family?
Don't you remember Carl Humbolt's boy
that was all twisted and deformed?
Him and that boy both's been dead for years
but people would go out there at night
when something had them torn all to pieces
(some of them real close to the edge)
and ask to see that little boy.
Carl would let them go in the back
where the boy would be on a pallet

(they were scared he'd fall off a bed)
and they'd get him to open his eyes
and look at who come to see him.
Then he'd reach out and they'd touch him
on his hands or the top of his head
and he would groan and whine
like he was taking it all on himself.
Carl said that every time he did it
it twisted him just a little more
but talked like this was his purpose. . .
Guess we'll never know if it was
but there's a few still around here
who swear by that boy."

The bell rang and Webb got up
and cranked the handle on the pump
causing the bubble propeller to flutter
as the conversation died forever
with the words, "Hi-test or regular?"

Old Tales

So many of them have come and gone
never again to be resurrected
or accessed by a memory but lost
from the lips that told them last
like liquid beads on a tin dipper
that drip from a raised chin.

Some hold clues to life and death
or the keys to divining people
while some tout truths homespun
from the blend of many strings
with such morals woven through
as to be deemed wise or timeless.

Of all that shame or grace or guide
there is one through which a lens
of insight opens on those older
and by which newer ones are read
if there is to be communion
with any story's life and power.

Do not miss this feast for fools
by being one and gorging on
the wine and bread brought first
when more has been prepared.
Save room! And do not miss
the tale within the tale.

Seeing the Elephant

I wasn't there the day the wheels
squeaked from Kingsport to Erwin
and the rails cried out their distress
while bearing the weight of the elephants
featured in Sparks World Famous Shows
but I heard the tale of Mary
a large and sullen gray five tons
and how she led the smaller ones
stiff and nervous from their ride
and a hurried Kingsport matinee
through a gantlet of human flesh
to a cool soak in a nearby pond
and how she came to be diverted
in that parade up Center Street
by hogs in contest over watermelon rinds
which so aroused her jealousies
and kinked the progress trunk to tail
that her handler jabbed her with the goad
and thereby ended in a blink
a brief unpromising career.

She snatched him from her back
as one would pluck a loathsome bug
and flexed up high above her head
before slamming him and breaking him
against a wooden soft drink stand
then calmly stepping on his head
and bearing down with weight enough
to pop it like a sour grape
and excite the crowd into a frenzy
as she stood bold and unrepentant

listening to the others trumpet defiance
and scattering headlong in the blare
a throng of panic-stricken patrons
who saw more in that moment's horror
than all the shows on earth could bring
and found themselves spurred by fear
to push and shove and trip their way
to a safer sideline distance
where righteous indignation took control
and cried out for something to be done.

By the time the tents were folded
and the train chugged into Erwin
groaning with its awesome double burden
the word had traveled down the line
like a surge of electric current
as far as Johnson City's gilded spires
and all the way to Rogersville
where town officials at both places pledged
to thwart the progress of this grim train
on which a demon beast was poised
to propagate her violent crimes
and bugle victory over those she crushed
and outraged citizenry at its worst
whipped to a froth by wild reports
vowed death to the crazed behemoth
more sinister than Romeo or Hannibal
or any other rogue of circus fame
demanding the price be fully paid
and the murderous rampage ended
and their own sensitivities avenged.

In the soft drizzle of that afternoon
amid persuasions from a growing throng
they took her to the railroad yard
and placed a chain around her neck
while she swayed back and forth
as if rooted to that one spot
and hooked it to the steel ring
that dangled from a derrick boom
then pulled it taut and lifted her
as they would a locomotive engine
until a weakened link gave way
and caused her bulk to drop
and one massive hip to break
sending panic through a nervous crowd
poised like Levites at a crucifixion
to cut and run from holy wrath
and would have if a roustabout
with a larger stretch of chain
had not performed the ritual again
and hanged her a second time.

I was not standing up the line
where they dropped her in the hole
and covered her body over with dirt
there in the Clinchfield yard
or when they went back in the dark
and dug her gray mass up again
to cut away the ivory tusks
but I have stood by impotent
while a brood sow ate her young
as chilled and mesmerized as others
by the curiosities of rage and pain
and I have witnessed all the inhumanities
all the atrocities and crimes
goaded and paraded for amusement's sake
strong men made to break like twigs

by the weak who gloat and strut
children made to suffer torment
and women turned into stone
and in these clearer revelations
I have seen the elephant.

Seeing the Elephant: The story of the elephant hanging in
Erwin, Tennessee on 9-13-1916 is told in the volume *The Day They
Hung the Elephant,* by Charles Edwin Price (Overmountain Press,
1992). It is based on eyewitness accounts of the incident and contains
a photograph of the hanging. Hannibal and Romeo were other circus
elephants who had killed their handlers.

Stomping Ground

No matter how we go
or how long it has been
the invitation always holds
to visit who we were
and live the laughter over
and breathe the smells again
redreaming for a little while
whole worlds we made and left.

We are always being born
to these same old places
coming back after long intervals
to see them as they were
and finding memory at odds
with what they have become
yet knowing all the while
it is we who have diminished.

Cat Heads

It got to be a ritual
each year's sacrifices building on the last
as the inauguration of dog days
spelled disaster for all house cats
feared to have touches of distemper
at the slightest wheeze or running sore
and verified if human ministrations
resulted in a scratch or bite.
They would be shot as acts of charity
amid gestures of feigned reluctance
and buried near the ditch bank
or at the yard's moist edge
or under ashes by the washpot
or out behind the flower box
but if someone listened long enough
to the county agent's radio report
and someone almost always did
they would have to be unearthed
and distastefully but dutifully exhumed
ordinarily after three to five days
with heads severed from their spines
and taken in a plastic bag or box
to the far-away state hospital
for careful medical examination.

Ours was a yard full
of hapless headless cats
at rest in the dips and shallows
marked only by some slight depression
or a bald spot in the grass
or whatever little pebble borders
that children deemed appropriate

and remembered throughout youth
as the place where Stripe was buried
or the grave of the bob-tail Whiskers
all the more difficult to eulogize
or immortalize without their heads.
Millennia perhaps eons from now
when all that remains of us
is embedded in a layer of shale
and some shimmering higher being
takes sample borings with a core drill
and subjects them to a carbon dating
what will be made of this find
of feline fossils without crania?
Will it be labeled a religious rite
or a crude genetical experiment?
Primitive cryonics or one of those
unsolved mysteries of the ancients?

Hired Help

Home from the Navy during WWII
in his old spot on the porch
he unfolded the thick Sunday paper
to catch the latest war news
only to be joined by Hugh
who helped out around the place
but who could not read nor write
a stigma that did not prevent him
from picking up an unused section
not knowing it was upside down
and commencing to read the news.

Each time the sailor turned a page
Hugh would look on and follow suit
each time a brow raised or furrowed
his own would mimic a response
until it became a mild irritant
for the one on thirty-day leave
who rose to announce he'd finished
just as Hugh eyed the inverted ship
on his remaining page and said
"I see here where a boat turned over!"
and rose with similar importance.

Slaying the Dragon

It used to be
that when the beast would come
breathing fire and shimmering
through a shroud of putrid smoke
intent on devouring all it could
there would appear a champion
skylined on the solitary plain
and he would stand across its path
with nothing but an iron resolve
to rid its menace from us.
He would not wilt before its flames
or evade the thrashing tail
or otherwise stand down
but would wait in great patience
as it stamped and roared and circled
rippling its great silver scales
then swiftly pick his moment
and plunge the sword in deep
and still its raging heart.

But in our time
when heroes fall and die
and old eyes out of habit
still look across the barren plain
it comes in ways more sinister
sometimes lurking just below the skin
sometimes behind a rib
and its appetite is not assuaged
until it feeds on everything.
Just when the hour is darkest

and all seems desperate or lost
a woman steps into a room
to arrange the shields of lead
and activate an ionized beam
that slays this evil sleeping thing
gorged with our lives and interests
and burns its nest and eggs
while we lie upon metal tables
and she will be our champion.

Traders

When Seth's old gray mule died
he dragged it off to the back side
and sorrowed for it a few days
before walking three farms over
to buy the one he'd seen advertised.
He checked it good and led it home
deciding to hook up that afternoon
and make a turn through the pea field
but that mule paid him no mind
and crisscrossed the rows at will
dragging him off toward the woods
where it ran square into a tree
despite his hollering and jerking the lines.

Leading it back as the warm sun
slanted off toward clouds in the west
and birds and insects gave subtle hints
commensurate with the waning day
he handed the reins to the owner
and allowed how he could not trade
due to the fact the mule was blind
relating it down to the last detail.
The owner gave off a grin and said,
"That mule ain't blind! I raised it!"
then placed a hand on Seth's shoulder
confiding that the mule's problem was
it just didn't give a damn.

Beekeepers

His father moved among the hives
encumbered by the shade of hat and veil
and thick padding head to toe
gloved hands working the smoker
and confusing little denizens on guard
at the triangular holes of entry.

Each heavy dripping frame would go
into the white enameled dishpan
and be borne like golden treasure
through a cloud of whirring wings
to the safety of the screened porch
and packed in blue Mason jars.

It was the old way
that knew only how to rob
and leave enough for winter food
but never ventured far beyond
saving the extra beeswax
or catching an errant swarm.

The son outstripped his father's pride
in the last university year
rendering him pathetic and outdone
in his old padded costume
as he spoke in condescending terms
of methods cold and intervening.

All marveled when he brought the box
with the stamped laboratory proof marks
and boldly inaugurated the requeening
smearing the remains of the old one

on the sugared prison of the new
so the others would accept her

Explaining how all such messages
were telegraphed by smell
and how repeated puffs of smoke
would disrupt and subdue each hive
so that the keeper had no care
and needed no protection.

As he rounded out his lecture
to those who listened from the porch
and put the final super back in place
bareheaded and in shirt sleeves
and looking perfectly at home
in the brown buzzing cloud

An inbound worker flecked with dust
from the far-off clover fields
flew into the closing crack
just as the wood pinched down
eradicating life and limb
but not the telepathic scent.

The pheromone sent out messages
at a speed surpassing thought
and changed a docile gathering
into a raging stinging swarm
which struck its troubler full force
with pain from a thousand barbs.

A helpless family watched in awe
as the poison swelled his heart
and slowly closed his airway
affording him the stunned surprise
of being cradled close in death
by padded and outdated arms.

A Dirge of the Land

Whatever happened to those old smiling farms
that grinned like waving grandparents
from the banks of unpaved county roads
with ladders to the haymaws of their barns
askew and clinging to a single nail
and proud bantams scratching their insignias
in the worked-over powder of the yards?
What happened to the ripe sunburned fields
with their leaning posts and rusting wire
and old broken-down peach orchards
gray from the drill rings of the peckerwoods
bereft and skeletal in a flurry of crows?

If they have survived the unkind times
as prisoners of the briar and privet hedge
there is some slim chance of rescue
but as they go the way of trailer parks
or softball fields or subdivided lots
and are scraped away and planed away
to link the sprinklers to the driving range
or lay the culverts to the shopping mall
all character and memory will be erased
and there will live upon the land
the great and groundless themes of flesh
which have no cause to celebrate themselves.

Living To Tell It

There was not half the effort spent
wrestling a thirty-pound catfish
from the mud-slick bottom of his pond
and bringing it to the bank
in a boil of brown foam
as there was casually hauling it about
in the flat of a wagon bed
mentally calculating those timed stops
at the key places in town
and taking extra pains to see
that every disbeliever got a look.

It was dark when he dressed it
by the lamp on the back porch
ringed by a host of moths and millers
and the glass eyes of the house cats
taking his time around the fins
observing from their reddened flush
that the signs were in the tail
then spilling out the entrails
engorged beyond their normal size
and opening the bloated stomach sac
to find a baby's arm inside.

After a brief sojourn in the kitchen
to say the meat had spoiled
his voice sounding strange and hollow
like someone speaking in a dream
he buried it by the hog lot
along with what had been removed
his mind keeping cadence with the spade

while wondering how a child that small
could end up being food for fish
without some small assistance
and figuring it to be a woman's work.

He could not bring himself to share
this finding with a solitary soul
but wrote it on a scrap
and tucked it in his Bible
back there in the book of Luke
where it lay untouched and yellowed
until that final feeble spring
when he took to the sickbed
and watched the mantle clock so much
he asked his wife to find the Book
and read him something from it.

She fished it from a cluttered drawer
deciphering his faint request
to find the part about Peter's mother
lying sick with a fever
and listening to his labored breath
pant faster as the pages turned
then picked up the dated scrap
that marked the story's place
and boldly read the words aloud
before stopping midway through
to throw up her hands and scream.

Immigrants

Their long lines streamed for a decade
from vessels in the Charleston port
crowding docks with their baggage and music
crinkled men fastened to stub pipes
whose backs were forever turned on Antrim
gaunt women with their litters of *get*
spread out like ragged clothes on a line
cuffed and knocked about and curtly told
to buck up and hold fast to one another.

These were those who refused to lie down
in fresh-made graves on the Emerald Isle
like so many of their kith and kin
with hearts starving in the specter's shadow
of the second great potato famine
and hopes driven like square-headed nails
into the coffins of the tender young
who never got to hold or bite the crust
of the shining dream called America.

Ten who took to the wagon roads
and a place called the Lower Long Canes
cast their meagerness among old Presbyterians
mending shoes in the dead of summer nights
after bending their backs in sunlit fields
saving the precious coppers in string bags
to go against the day they raised up
house and shed with nothing left to spare
but two dressed boards of heart pine.

Immigrants: The immigrant James William MaGill (1797-1853) came with his wife and eight children from Larne, County Antrim, Ireland, in 1842. The family settled in that part of the Abbeville District of South Carolina which became McCormick County. MaGill and wife Margaret McFall are buried in the Lower Long Canes Presbyterian Cemetery in unmarked graves. While they came in poverty, their family became prominent after two generations.

Leviathan

Sometimes it comes from our depths
weltering without pity or compassion
in the narrow troughs of our blood
like it did that day in Rhunelle
about to balance to the penny
on her tape at the teller window
in the Sun Trust Bank of Ramah
and close the vault on another weekend
complete with its physical discomforts
for those who bore the monthly mark
reserved for creatures of her gender.

She was three days into her cycle
chewing gum and fighting cramps
and smarting from the glib demeanor
of a younger teller named Layona
who had simply glanced at her sideways
when a ne'er-do-well named Slick Haynie
not long since incarcerated for theft
burst in with shotgun and ski mask
and swiftly singled out Rhunelle
in her rhinestone glasses and chains
and started screaming in her face.

He hopped over the lower counter
and forced Layona and her balding boss
to lie face-down on the wood tiles
while Rhunelle filled his paper bag
with what was in the cash drawer
pale and fearful for her life
as he shouted it was not enough
and pushed both barrels of that gun
deep against her upper abdomen
triggering a wave of wracking pain
that broke and bent her double.

Rising on the swells of a rage
born in the lochs of ancient myth
she first smoothed out her skirt
and lured him into the open vault
past a doorway of scalloped steel
and the metal ribs of her lair
on the promise of more inside
then eased the door with one hand
while pointing to the bulging sacks
until it clicked and shut behind them
leaving him to her dark mercies.

After twenty soundproof minutes
the vault was sprung by armed police
with every weapon trained inside
then quickly lowered before Rhunelle
hair flying and both arms flailing
clutching half-filled bags of pennies
and pounding them with a vengence
into the thick skull of Slick Haynie
whimpering in a puddle of his making
and dragged out with five Abe Lincolns
permanently embossed on his forehead.

As the clamor and excitement died
and those lately sensitized by fear
pitched in to clean up the place
words were kept to a minimum
and eyes hardly left the floor
as Rhunelle tried to make the change
back to who she'd always been
but those who saw it taking place
were not deceived by her feigned attempts
remembering a beast she had called forth
who surely lived and lurked within.

Old Man Mose

Children dreaded his coming
for it meant the end of something
a cow down from a bad birth
or a horse grown old and lame
or a favorite hound with distemper.
He would lead them off
or drag them with a tractor
to the far end of a pasture
and that would be the end of them.

As dreaded as the Plague
he had those kind but killing eyes
you hoped he'd never turn on you
but keep focused on the hog killings
or the perpetual chicken slaughters
when the pens were emptied out
and the yard ran red with blood
and headless fowl in silent flopping
pumped their own hearts dry.

No one followed him off
when he took a tied sack of kittens
from those too squeamish to do it
and headed for the highway bridge
or the night he came for Julie's pups
with us bunched around the dinner table
listening to her howl at the night

long after he made off with them
and the world had gone to bed.

And no one could forget his eyes
so moist and brown and sympathetic
or that look of reverence and respect
that viewed us with God's pity
but that hid a killer's heart.
Sometimes in the dead of night
years after the wheel has turned
I close my eyes and see him
and wonder when he'll come for me.

Snow in the South

Snow in the South
puts a new look on the landscape
like the brick home going up
with all the modern conveniences
in sight of the old ramshackle one
with the leaning backyard privy
which is destined to be torn down
once the old woman is ready
to say goodbye and make the change.
He has built it for her
as the last bold public act
of his often unexpressed affections
bringing tools out of retirement
and taking all the foolhardy risks
that hang from gable ends and ladders
satisfied at the day's end
but sitting by the old oil stove
staring at his swollen feet
and wondering if he'll live to finish it.

Snow in the South
makes everything strange at first
like those rooms with low ceilings
in which nothing seems to fit
and the inexpressible quiet
of feet unaccustomed to carpet
and the white daylight brightness
of fluorescents at the kitchen sink.
She will be long amazed by it
and pleased that he will not care
how cold the winters are
if he has to get up at night
but she has seen beyond his smiles
the length to which he pushes
hearing the hammering after dark

and watching exhaustion take its toll
and she does not want to spend
a day alone inside and know
that this is what has killed him.

Snow in the South
clings to a few shaded spots
long past the thaw and melt
like the last long look
of a man about to die
cast back upon the house
after going down the steps
gray-faced and laboring for breath
to make the final doctor's trip
from which there would be no return.
Steadying on the open car door
and peering from a weathered husk
that once was so invincible
his eyes behold what he has made
appraising every board and brick
laid by his hands with a love
for which there was no words
and in those hard-earned moments
all things unresolved fall into place.

Snow in the South
is like a wish at Christmas
that falls into disrepair
only to get wished over
or the stubborn shining dream
that floats above the bed
in the last fading of the day
and gets reclaimed and revisited
after the family has left
and the room falls back to sleep
and the halls shrink to a whisper.
It will beat the pulse in him
long after the recognition ceases

and the memories all run through
and there is little else to do
but lie there as it hovers
keeping a lone and intimate vigil
until the machines give him up
and it can open its flower to him.

Far Fields

The look in the eyes of the dying
if not from the morphine drip
is that of faraway fields
caught all along in glimpses
but never owned until the end
when those standing around the bed
can look into a wrinkled face
and see the boy or girl
who waits until then to go there.

Death Knell

She was lured there by those letters
which kept all the promises intact
light and fanciful and interceding
inviting her at age sixteen
to leave her father's Carolina home
and move down to McRae
around the time the century turned
to share an almost perfect world
and tie the blessed blissful knot
and gain in the same good bargain
a whitewashed clapboard house
with hanging baskets and green shutters
gleaming in its clean-swept yard
and purple martins diving from the gourds
to catch the unsuspecting swarms
winging by its window flower boxes.

It was too powerful an urge
for a heart that tender to resist
and so she fed on every line
then went those solitary miles
through a frenzy of harsh elements
and the endless zig-zag wagon ruts
to be a willing bride for him
and stayed for over thirty years
cooking meals and giving birth
and eking out a meager livelihood
in the same pinched tar paper shack
that all but spoiled her glad arrival
sullen and sitting off to itself

near a vine-choked spur of the railroad
where only occasional turpentine hands
would pass and tip the hat.

She was there in nineteen eighteen
when the influenza took its toll
and homemade coffins large and small
waited by the tracks in record numbers
for shipment somewhere down the line
and she faced the Great Depression
and its gaunt and hollow-eyed minions
from the hearth of a scorched fireplace
squatting by the crude Dutch oven
for light enough to read those letters by
and reminisce about the early days
when she had first turned the pages
that promised her heaven on earth
while sitting in the front porch swing
bright and wistful and childlike
doting on each glad detail.

She would visit when she could
on brief infrequent trips at first
to acquaint the children with their kin
and then on long extended jaunts
each time the elderberry bloomed
and the mimosa spread its plumes
and she would breathe in smells
and drink in sights and solitudes
that flooded all the sensibilities
with the euphoria of coming home
knowing that the hour would come
for dragging those long miles back
to face the grim necessities

of his tired and weathered world
bereft of the soft-spun winsome dreams
each loving letter had described.

When he died in later life
and the great rush of the years
yielded as part of their sparse harvest
an aged form grown gray and slight
she enjoyed extended intervals
back at her childhood home
with hopes of being buried there
but when that great translation came
her daughter took the body to McRae
to be placed alongside his
and as it rested by the grave
and after final words were said
she had it opened one last time
and took that long departing look
and tucked those letters down inside
before they gently closed the lid.

Stations in Hell

Take old man Moss, for instance
owned all that property
and never once went out of doors
to stretch his legs upon it
or stop to mark a corner
yet plastered those signs on the trees
and dared the likes of you and me
to set a foot across or cut
so much as a riding switch

or that one who forever cursed his kids
and beat them to a fare-thee-well
you could hear them hollering
clear over to our place
made them work when they were sick
from the oldest to the least
but the law never touched him
even when his little six-year-old
dropped dead in the cotton fields

or Lucille out on the Gresham place
a regular blue-vein throbber
who got the boys so worked up
two of them fought over her
swapping vicious words and licks
until a hunting knife was pulled

and hefted into one dead-center
it taking prison and an early grave
to prove she wasn't worth it.

There are more than these
and you could rightly name them all
as they float up to the top
in our smokes and recollections
and if there is a special place
reserved to house each one
they need to give us latitude
to pick who sits or stands
who gets burnt or beat or flayed.

Touch of Frost

He set out plants in March
risking the early spring freezes
to gain a growing edge
and be held in high esteem
by neighbors less inclined
than he to chance the weather.

She watched him from the porch
despising the singular attention
he lavished on the plants
there being none for her
as she weathered more each year
like the clapboards on the house.

The night before a chilling frost
sure to burn the tender green
he stooped to cover them all
shielding each one in paper bags
anchored by clods and rocks
to stand against the wind.

On her way to the privy
long after he had gone to bed
she went out into the rows
and moved the make-shift weights
holding down the buffeted bags
to let them blow away.

The wind laid shortly after
and white crystals formed a crust
on every farm and field
stinging life from his plants
and joy from his breast
as she had hoped it would.

How well the adage holds
that some toil through the day
to plant the flower of purpose
while some labor in the night
sowing seeds of vengence
and yield a better harvest.

Stone Soup

It has been hell getting out of the cave
up from red meat
and taking what we want
but we have fought and clubbed our way
to picnics and recitals
and earned the right to sit in meetings
or stand in crowded terminals
forever looking at our wrists.

Oh, the skulls we crushed to get here
the veins we bled
the reasons we invented
which have all but licensed us
to arrive at these places
where drinks are served
and bridge is played
and feel the prick of little deaths.

Eighth Sister

On one of those late November mornings
the stone for which was a topaz
that matched the eyes of cats
she sat alone without a light
in the quietness of a house
grown colder over eighty years
surrounded by familiar things
that seemed somehow less than hers
staring through the window pane
at the sumac waving its red pennants
from the stubble of the ditch bank
and wondering who would come for her.

She remembered picking up the sticks
under the oak in the front yard
head covered by an old silk kerchief
halved and tied under her chin
to ward off the damp and chill
but there was no memory to explain
how she got halfway to town
loitering through the lawns confused
until someone coaxed her into a car
and made the brief trip back
and used her phone to make the call
that told how she had wandered off.

That night she dreamed it once again
the warm wide hands of her father
on her shoulders as a girl
pointing out a host of constellations
glittering above the fields at night
and teaching her their names
their vast and varied mythic shapes

while picking out her favorite one
called Pleiades or The Seven Sisters
and saying that when it was time
she would go up and take her place
and shine as one among them.

The next few weeks were wanderings
in a wilderness of jumbled thoughts
with doctors probing for dementia
and asking her the day and time
with strangers sitting in her house
usurping her at every turn
and pilfering cabinets and drawers
under the guise of looking after her
causing her to make a quiet retreat
into the soft dark inner reaches
with a vague recollection that her name
had been placed on a waiting list.

By year's end all she ever was
had been uprooted and given over
to the Fairview Nursing Home
to strange smells and shattered cries
of aimless souls who stalked the halls
reaching out in their imaginations
only to find her at a transom
looking up toward a piece of darkness
spangled by faint pinpoints of light
shining down on this one waiting form
with arms outstretched and palms open
ready to be recognized and taken up.

Through the Needle's Eye

How do they run day and night
and not stop to catch their breaths
the slim hounds
sleek and spare and tireless
with no meat on the shoulderbone
and no fat along the ribs
just the sheen of red and brown
down the hills of green and brown
and up the other side
like a blur of madness
in and out of hearing
chasing life from the flashing fox
light and fleet and flowing
harried and hunted hard
chasing life from the winded fox
and running it to the ground?

The horn that blows them back and forth
across the splashing streams
and along the velvet banks
the horn that knows the range of notes
the long-range scatter and drift
that rides the layered currents
and guides their flawless grace
is from the lips of one who sounds
clear on the breaking day
or muted in the waxing of the moon
the cleaving in the checkered maze
the hidden window in the hedge

and a way through briar and thorn
as they run on silent feet --
feet made swift and sure
tracing a golden thread.

With the day flown and fast dying
its life lagging and far-spent
narrowing and narrowing the earth
held fast in tightening thickets
to that single sky-swept spot
they come through sunlit shafts
through eyelets of gold and emerald
down a worn and shining path
to be delivered and retrieved
the chains snapped to their collars
as they wait warm and trembling
with no strike on their countenance
to tell where they have been
over and under the whisper of fields
in and about the ringing hollows
around and through the shrouded dens.

Yard Sale

In placing on the table
old tie-dyed shirts and outgrown jackets
and the last of the plastic toys
she has agreed to make for sale
these few surviving family pieces
saying mental and emotional farewells
and letting them go like children
beyond the boundaries that once defined
their strict and guarded ownership.

The last bicycle and skateboard
and the sprawling two-tiered dollhouse
forever swept around and stumbled over
since that Christmas twenty years ago
are among the aging keepsakes
along with the old heavy coffee mugs
and some early marriage cookware
but she felt compelled to tag the lot
and get on with her life.

When strangers come and take it
leaving her their loose change
and a small sheaf of folding green
she will be free of the clutter
but her heart will know the anguish
of a great and staggering betrayal
made more painful by the urge
to rid from memory the remains
of all that made her who she is.

Freak Show

It is one thing to stand there
in front of raucous crowds
and pierce the skin with needles
or hang weights from a human tongue
dislocating limbs and swallowing fire
in these one-stop traveling shows
but it is a different game
to be the one who pays
to witness the disfigurement of flesh
or watch a body writhe in pseudo-anguish
and be completely entertained.

Those some generations back
with lesser means but greater hearts
would not have paid to be amused
by base anatomical displays
of spasm and contortion
but were it in their power
to intervene in such performances
they would lay hold of these abominations
and take them out into a shed
and beat the daylights out of them
or lock them in some dark back room.

Making Sure

In separate village houses beat
these hearts of gaiety and warmth
but there is one on third street
which held a hard chill in its hallway
one raw winter night in forty-three
when the body of the eldest son
brought in a bag from North Africa
rested in its box of dark mahogany
sealed with long screws at the corners.

You could blow frost in that hallway
where a uniformed guard kept vigil
under orders to stand the night's watch
and to disallow a private viewing
or removal of the flag-draped coffin lid
despite a grieving father's earnest plea
for one quick, identifying look
in order to prove beyond a shadow
that the boy inside was his.

It was well past the stroke of twelve
when the smell of fresh-brewed coffee
and the mention of a layer cake
mixed with the flattery of womenfolk
and lured the soldier into bright warmth
while father and son came like ghosts

and bent themselves to a grisly task
screwdrivers turning in protesting wood
to whispers of, "Be quick about it!"

Once beyond the groan made by the lid
and the slit made in the canvas bag
they found a charred and blackened corpse
burned beyond the faintest recognition
whereupon they worked in frantic haste
to pry and pull the frozen jaw apart
cutting the stitching through the mouth
and inserting their screwdrivers as wedges
then using one for leverage.

By the light of a kitchen match
the father scraped at the lower molars
until a gleam from a metal filling
revealed the old starburst pattern
on the one cracked and crooked tooth
more telling than a fingerprint
yet numbing for the two who saw
and who would see it from then on
each time they closed their eyes.

Leper Colony

Shipped by night on a coal barge
to a state-appointed wilderness
they were made to stay there
in a forgotten bend of the Mississippi
and mill about without treatment
aimless in their desolation
their only manual Leviticus
chapter thirteen verse forty-five
their only prospect for a change
the same paradise afforded thieves
as they lived out the letter of the Law
from a daily psychic admonition
pronouncing them, "unclean, unclean."

The Sisters of Mercy gave them little
beyond the treatment of their sores
further separating them by sex
until isolation was complete
and they forgot each other's shapes
and no longer mattered to themselves
but with the scourge of passing years
as skin and tissue fell away
and fingers went down to the nubs
and the shadow of despair looked back
like a bony specter in a cowl
from the gleam of every empty plate
time ate the remaining crumbs.

For eleven sore and misspent seasons
as others of their kind were rounded up
and herded in ragged random droves
to this home within the wilderness
this piece of scuffed and tainted ground

chafed and flecked from their contamination
and known derisively by some
as the Ostrich Farm or Leper Land
the heart would strain against its chains
and life would curse its solitary lot
the soul would lift its anguished howl
and raise its raging pleas aloft
till someone finally heard its prayers.

Leper Colony: The National Hansen's Disease Center at Carville, Louisiana, was not established until 1921, though victims of the disease were legally incarcerated there by the state by 1894 and were not adequately housed until 1906. Public attitude and national policy regarding the apprehension and detention of leprosy victims did not change until 1956, and as late as 1978, detention laws were on the books. The Center closed in 1999 because of improvements in the treatment of the disease. See: Vicki E. Pannell, "Social Policy for Hansen's Disease in the United States." 8-1-1985. 14 pp; *USA Today.* 1-8-1999. p. 11A.

Cargo

On these scheming nights
thoughts billow like sails
straining against tight grinding hemp
run loose like dogs let out
to sic themselves on anything
that breathes or moves.
These are hard-fought brooding nights
for twisted flights of love or crime
for bold neurotic signatures
stitched inside shirts and coats
by those shipping out at dawn
niches for all the righteous moves
the recollected joys and hurts
fermenting in sweltering holds
of remorse and self-abasement
poultices for blood-red indulgences
lodged upon the hanging reefs
and left to groan like derelicts.

These are restless seething nights
in which prisoners on their beds
poised for the breaking moment
court the edge and count the waves
in which care laces the veins
with its paralyzing explanations
for every little hairline flaw
and the assaults of age and death
wring out the salt and starch
and leave their malarial stench.
These are nights to swear by

to taste the brass of dreams by
with their herringbone patterns
that set things right or ill
nights to lie awake by
in the shark-infested darkness
waiting for the darting loneliness
to hone in for the kill.

At the Candlelite Motel

It was in the last lingerings
of a day reddened and far-spent
in the dying time of August
with the sun bleeding like a sieve
in the middle of the road
when Bunny totaled register receipts
and cut the outside neons on
and stuck out the battered placard
with its faded red arrow
so that guests and late arrivals
could find the outside buzzer
once she closed up for the night.

She hoped to skip the night desk
with only six rooms booked
and shower and turn in early
if the mermaid down in number five
running out all the hot water
would condescend to turn it off
and the pack of gypsies camped in two
did not roam the grounds all night
and disturb her sleeping patrons
and if the tire salesman in eight
would hang up the office line
and leave off the smooth talk.

She sprayed some cleanser in a rag
and wiped off the counter top
watching the dust motes hang in air
burnished on the thick pink shafts
streaming through the venetian blinds
like prison bars across the room
and tinting the old brother-sister pose
of her with her arm around Gene

thumbtacked to the cork board
causing her throat to ache
as she caught herself remembering
how sundown was his favorite time.

After changing to a housecoat
and switching on that game show
she stood at the bathroom mirror
listening to the overhead pipes
complain about the water being on
and inspecting the spidery crevices
new and detectable about the eyes
so different from the flawless face
shining in the Senior photograph
that matched her ageless twin
but high school was a distant dream
flown on the wings of years.

The car pulled up at dusk
just as she took the last look out
and parked under the roadside neons
facing the last of the faint pink
a two-door fifty-seven Chevy
turquoise with a light cream top
like the one her brother drove
through those green and white reflectors
off the high end of Ray's Bridge
on a night too deep to fathom
with a life too young to hazard
gone twenty years next June.

She froze behind the plate glass
peering through the cold cream
amazed by what came back
the ducktail cut, the aftershave
the fifties tunes they both enjoyed
sitting right there on summer nights
and watching the sun go down

66

as he blew those lazy rings
one after another out the window
and rocked the large foam dice
hanging from the rear-view mirror.
God, this looked a lot like Gene!

She had to find out who it was
and went back to her room to change
but by the time she washed her face
and dressed and went outside
the first faint stars were out
and the object of her fascination gone.
Walking over to the familiar spot
like a form made of clay or wood
she knelt down for the longest
by a fresh pair of skid marks
stunned but trying to catch again
the one-time whiff of lemon-lime.

Learned in Rain

With the advent of each raindrop
as it forms and falls and shatters
in increments or at once
and as one flight among many
there is a moment grasped
then justified as having been;
singular yet related to the rivulets
that move it toward the whole.
It can no more be kept
than one can trace the genealogy
of a single silver needle
thinned and honed by wind
as it takes a thousand shapes
before touching thirsty earth
or striking among stones
to be freed as vapor
or formed as ice.
Such are life's moments
driven by the tumult of forces
and sunk like hammered nails
into the flesh of God
all joys and agonies descending
in the great giving-over
of selves too numerous to count
to universal sighs and urges
which recite as one voice
the myths of individuation.

Reflections on Snow Hill

What possessed you, little flock
to acquiesce and stray so far
lured away from the deep longing
that birthed such childlike faith
and marked this as a sacred spot
where cares and rivalries were put aside
and harmony gave leave for all
to sit at the feet of Jesus?
What great temptations blowing through
carried like spores on the wind
enticed you to forsake the larger fold
and constitute yourselves another way
breaking a chain of everlasting friendship
that once draped these silent groves.

The elders encamped long before you
asleep for a century upon this hill
through threadbare Octobers
in the great and stretching silence
never once believed their pledge of faith
could be so swiftly overturned
or that the righteousness and power
pouring out of Immanuel's veins
would ebb with total dissolution
back into this common field of strife
where everything in nature waits
for the pains and the pleasures
for the droughts and the floods
for the cold and the sun.

Reflections on Snow Hill: Snow Hill Congregational Methodist Church (1917) in Wilkinson County, Georgia, was formed from a split with Laurel Branch Methodist Episcopal Church, South (1848). The new church was built across from the McCook Cemetery, long used by the Methodist Episcopal Church and the Methodist Episcopal Church, South, prior to their split in 1844. Many ministers from the McCook family served in these entities before and after their reuniting in 1939. The Congregational Methodist Church, formed in Georgia in 1854, never merged back into the united body of Methodism.

Dark Thirty

The evening Tommy hanged himself
by kicking out the folding chair
he'd used to fasten the noose
to one of the white I-beams
at the back of Dexter's body shop
he heard the high pitched notes
ringing in the outside lot
and the ball smacking the building
causing him to find the high window
with its rich deepening velvet
and wish for those quick exhilarations
that fueled the play at first dark.

He should have been out there
charged with the after-dinner renewal
that brought forth amazing bursts
as the street lights winked on
and the tired and old and docile
slipped quietly to their beds
but for this one children's hour
he had come out from among them
to situate himself aloft and purified
stomach empty and head light
fed only by the fledgling hope
that he would not soil himself.

It had been a stolen afternoon
and he had been a willing thief
filling it with things forbidden
like the rifle from the closet
he was told never to touch
and he had stood up with it
in the front of his father's boat

at the dock on Wilson's landing
shooting the fish in the shallows
so intent on mastering the angle
he lost his balance in the boat
and shot a hole in its bottom.

An act so wrong and unforgivable
lent wings to self-destructive prayers
that begged for swift, magical release
from this and other adolescent claims
at war with waning innocence
and he had gone the further step
with a purloined safety razor
and shaved off the pubescent hair
so alien to the boy he'd been
and flushed it without a trace
before taking his father's spare key
and entering through the paint room.

It felt so good to stand there
by taped chrome and mirrored hoods
breathing in the thinner's ether
relieved never to have to know
a plethora of tasks and tools
and the great and grim bewilderments
that greeted every growing child
who played so unaware at dark
among the raucous singing crickets
and never heard the chair collapse
or saw his body swing and sway
held by a good Scout knot.

Dear and Wishful Heart

The tenderness in silent cribs
tucked beneath each fold of warmth
fragile in its dreamless infancy
can know no measure of compare

with eyes that have beheld the earth
from the pink tints of its morning
down to the last brush strokes
of its darkening browns and grays

with lips that have craved first
then curved themselves to taste and save
the inhalations of sweet scents
and slow exhales of soft delights

with longings that have surged
like the repressed hopes of children
on tiptoe at a threshold
poised to spill themselves inside

with love that has bestowed itself
in countless layers of gratitude
floating like oil on water
over the lingerings of each day

with joy enough to find at last
a place on Earth's firm pillow
where souls beckoned into sleep
are brushed by an angel's wing.

My Aunt Jett

Even with a body like Methuselah
creaking on old arthritic limbs
and a mind going back to the past
going back like taking dips
from the same rusted snuffbox
she's bound to give you something
like a notion or an insight
to carry home and use
if you're not too proud to take it.
Hear Aunt Jett . . .

On Whippin' Okra

"I got up one morning
weak as water in my legs and hands
at what I was about to do
but brave in my spirit
and I took me a broom handle
out among the tallest stalks
and I started whippin' that okra
crying when I cut it to pieces
like punishing children
to make them grow up to be good.
I grieved for it after that
propping it the night it rained
to keep it out of the mud
and in two weeks it bloomed
and the bent-over ones straightened
and I had okra until frost
which shows that whippin' anything
teaches it a good lesson
and it's better off for it!
Sometimes you got to whip it!"

On Lost Weeds

"Sudie knows what I'm talking about!
I told her she won't amount to much
going down to that clay bank
everyday like she always does
eating red mud and dotin'
on them old movie magazines.
They get her mind confused
so she don't look where she's going
and steps on a lost weed.
They grow everywhere all the time
and they will mess you up
so you can't find your way
even when you've been there
back and forth all your life.
You know how it is
when you come upon a place
only from a different side
and all of a sudden you stop
'cause you don't recognize it
and you take stock there and then
and have to mull it over
just as lost as a branch rabbit.
You done stepped on a lost weed!
Sudie does it all the time
but I ain't studying 'bout her!"

On Bang-Belly

"Boy, you don't know what hungry is
till you've had to go all day
busting up old hard red clods
with the back of a grubbin' hoe
like inching through broke glass.
You get right faint inside
feeling like you're going to pass

but you can make it all day
if your mama fills a sack
with them little flat hoecakes
that everybody used to call bang-belly.
They got made out of nothing
just wet corn meal and onions
fried in the leftover grease
and pressed out hard and flat
so they last out in the field.
I could go all day on two of them
and just sing and praise God
and never get so give-out weary
I'd have to blow or rest.
They would stick to you!"

On Po' Mouthin'

"My boy Lester comes in here
and he all the time telling me
how much he misses my cooking
and how he ain't been eating right
since I came to this rest home
and I tell him, 'Look here, Lester,
don't come in here po' mouthin'.
You near 'bout sixty years old
carrying on like somebody helpless!
You gonna have to see after yourself!'
But there's a world full just like him
ain't never had to break a sweat
or hit a lick at a snake!
Had it all handed straight to them
and they ain't give it a thought!
You think they'd be satisfied
but they go to whining and po' mouthin'
and you can't do nothing with them
no more than I can with Lester.
I tell him, 'Don't argue, child!

I know what I'm saying.
You can't keep leaning on a post.
It'll fall down after while.'"

On Cooking Collards

"It ain't enough to boil 'em!
First you got to pour off the brass
and it's your second water that rinses
and gives them that sweet taste!
Folks will tell you, 'Don't pour it off!'
like it's gonna rob you of the good
but what do they know?
Collards got more good in them
than a body could ever use up.
If you don't believe what I'm saying
eat 'em every day and see what they do.
Some folks eat 'em straight off
and don't wash them clean beforehand.
Me, I wash them to death!
Might near cook 'em to death, too!
And I put in a little fatback seasoning
to make them slick and tender
but that ain't all you need to know!
It don't matter how you cook collards
if they ain't had a touch of frost.
Frost makes a collard more fit to eat
than cooking ever thought about.
Don't let anybody tell you different!"

On Hants

"My mama was born
with a veil over her face
but she wasn't no hant!
When she died I was grown

77

and I was settin' up with her
and I got up in the night
crying and looking in the casket
and she opened her eyes and smiled
and said, 'Ain't you glad?'
but she wasn't no hant!
Hants are them that die troubled
and can't go on to rest
doomed to roam around here
mopin' and grievin' themselves over
whatever it is that's troublesome.
So if you die and ain't happy
you bound to have to travel
long past your natural time.
Don't plan on seeing Jesus
'til you walk a lot of road!"

On Storms and Such

"You can smell rain coming every time
just standing in the front door
and you can watch it come up the road
if you got a place to see it good!
But if it gets to thundering
and if the sky starts popping open
and showing you that devil's pitchfork
the best thing for you to do
is to sit in a corner and be quiet
while the Lord is doing his work.
You go to traipsin' around paying no mind
and He's liable to strike you graveyard dead!
He wants you to show Him some respect
because what He's bringing to the earth
you can't do and never will!
He took one of my sisters like that
when she was just a little girl

standing in the door with a comb
laughing and sticking out her tongue.
Killed her and bent that comb in two!
And after she was put in the grave
He sent down another bolt
and split the stone in two!
The Bible says that God is love
but He don't let nobody mock him
not even a child."

On Angels

"Not everybody can see 'em
and nobody can even glimpse them
unless they want you to.
There's a world of them out there
some on higher up the scale.
Angels and archangels get seen a lot
and they are the lowest there is.
Some got little red chevrons
stitched to their sleeves.
Them that carry swords are Principalities!
Dominions always carry swords, too
and they are always standing watch.
Flaming swords belong to the Powers
like the one that drove Adam out.
Thrones have got wheels of fire
and the only ones above them
are the Cherubim and Seraphim
who we get to see in heaven.
They don't come down here much!
If they do, you can't mess with them
can't see them, neither
but they'll be watchin' you!"

On The World

"The world's got you
and you don't know it!
People used to talk and sing
and now they've gone to grabbin'.
Church don't do them no good
they're grabbin' there, too!
The Lord's tired like me!
He's tired of all the grabbin'
and he's going to stop it, too!
Some people get polite in grabbin'.
They smile while they take it from you
like they've gone and helped you out.
They grab at me in here
roaming around this rest home
grabbin' at my clothes
and I ain't got nothin' with me
but this old beat-up rolling chair.
People ask me all the time
what I think and I say
It don't matter what I think!
This is the world!"

On Going to Heaven

"Everybody talking about it ain't goin'
'least that's what my old Pap said
and he trembled in his voice
when speaking about the judgment
'least that's what they tell me!
I know that he's gone there!
White folks all think they're goin'
and it's gonna to be like it is now
with them grinning and running everything
but they ain't nothing but a fool!
You don't mess with God!

He just as soon smite you
as look you in the face.
You got to fall down and humble yourself
if you want to be sanctified.
Ain't nobody goin' but them that is!
I hope God's gonna take me
but he fools lots of people.
Just cause you die don't always mean
that carriage is coming for you.
It's harder than you think it is
to turn your back on this world
and just sit and hope He'll take you.
You don't ever know!
Heaven's hard! It sho' is!"

A Fork Chronicle

The fire resurrected it
glazed and mottled in the ruins
and raked from between the chimneys
by cold tines stroking the spot
where it was poked between floorboards
by a child dead over a hundred years.

It was taken home and soaked
and dipped and buffed and rubbed
until its proofmark came to light
brought from a smudged indention
hidden on its flat underside
just above the graceful curve.

Once stored among its kind
in one of London's velvet drawers
spared from all but festive use
it came to occupy a plastic tub
filled with an odd assortment
being sold for a dollar each.

Passed over for eighteen seasons
as the rest were pawed and picked
it was spied and snatched one day
like a diamond from the rubble
by an inevitable bony hand
and held before a gleaming eye.

Soaked again and scalded
it finished out the set for one
who had looked high and low
and whose last lucid urge had been
to lay the perfect table with it
for her favorite guests but never did.

At death all was divided
between the distant nieces
who came together in a gaggle
and carried it to the four winds
scattering the pieces without thought
among their rude and witless kids.

Its fate was cast soon after
at a party off the Georgia coast
by raucous youngsters throwing ice
and spearing olives for a drink
on an already rolling deck
awash with spills of juice and gin.

A playful shove and it was launched
end over tarnished silver end
into the taupe-colored foam
to rest upon the cleansing sands
that ride the tug of tides
safe from unworthy hands.

To Listening Aliens

This is my earth, my moon
my night under it
like a child still-born
not mine to keep but mine
to call by names I choose
and mine to mourn.

If you have designs or claims
or curiosities far-flung
go find some distant place
less to my liking
and leave me to float
in this bubble of life.

I do not want enlightenment
more company, more choices
just let me process what I have
until I grow tired of it
or it tires of me
and buys my silence.

Windmill Hill

The annals will never reflect the way
Susannah set her cap for him
white teeth flashing a careless smile
and water dripping from the gourd
coaxing him from his duty in the tower
to be numbered among the duly smitten.
No sooner than he scurried down
a stalking shadow left the woods
to descend upon his Uncle Jed
planting corn in the short rows
far down the southeastern side
while he drank long and deep
squandering the life's blood of his kin.
The sound of the blow did not carry
as the axe buried itself in flesh
and the bucket tumbled down the hill
broadcasting yellow seed in wide spirals
'neath a row running rich with blood.
He got back to his perch in time
to see the black scalp being taken
and raised high as a trophy
while hot guilt pulled the bell rope
to raise a late and lame alarm.
That horror never left his eyes
nor those of Susannah's children
who passed it through five generations
where it looked out from the photograph
of one who never knew the story.

Windmill Hill: This property is situated about one half mile north of Inman, South Carolina, in Spartanburg County. Those first settling it were James W. Lawrence and his two brothers from Lunenburg County, Virginia, in 1791. The place marked an earlier border between white settlers and Indian territory where several disputes and massacres occurred.

Holy Ground

On the first night of a Holy Ghost revival
at the Gilgal Pentecostal Holiness Church
commonly called the church in the hole
due to the pitch of its shingled roof
being on level with the road grade
the Hudlow boys made their second pass
just as the front doors flew open
causing emotions that had been pent-up
for two righteous hours running
to rupture and spill forth into the yard
with joyous leaps and loud shouting
and arms raised up toward heaven.

When "My God, will you look at that!"
was exclaimed from the passenger side
and Bud Hudlow's eyes left the road
the ancient Plymouth crossed the line
and tagged someone's back fender
cartwheeling them across the asphalt
and slinging Cleet free and clear
then down the steep embankment
with the momentum of a spent bullet
and landing him in the churchyard
where he parted the crowd like Moses
and lay with open, outstretched arms.

He looked to be stone dead at first
but then there came a feeble twitch
that started in his right shoulder
and then a second and a third
as all stood back to watch him lurch
and jerk and writhe upon the ground

like a snake with its head run over
yet in perfect form and character
with the tenor of the faithful.
Someone shouted out, "Praise God!"
while witnessing the true conversion
of one who often mocked their ways.

A circle formed and people wept
laboring there in late-night prayer
and agonizing like Jesus over Jerusalem
while the Spirit did its mighty work
convulsing through its wayward son
and several shouted, "Out demons, out!"
The power was broken as a siren
scattered the throng left and right
and two attendants knelt beside Cleet
asking people to please step back
and calling out for a flashlight
as they wrestled with his thrashing form.

First one and then the other of them
drew back and slapped himself
then stood up to jump and shake
amid remarks like, "Glory to God!"
yet before these actions were attributed
to the quickening power of the Almighty
an eight cell beam was trained on Cleet
revealing hordes of fire ants boiling mad
and swarming from their flattened bed
dispelling all hopes of it being God's work
but who is there to say with certainty
that they were not His chosen instruments?

Chinaberry Wars

I am a veteran of the chinaberry wars
who slung my arm out throwing them
at those whose prowess proved to be
as formidable as the hosts of Midian
according to the red welts they raised
bouncing in torrents hard and green
off those of us less skilled but who were
nevertheless numbered among the righteous.
Our vindication came that same August
when too many of them climbed the tree
from which the stinging missiles came
pelting down upon our bare heads
like the plagues of hail and locust
yet the Lord saw fit to deliver us
from the vile mockery of our adversaries
by snapping the top branches
and raining our enemies down upon us
where we pummeled them without mercy
until they begged us to hold off
and sued for a lasting peace.

In the Line of Duty

Only a burned spot marked the grass
on that side of Highway 72
and it was gone by the next April
taking with it the only monument
to that fateful Wednesday in May
when a trooper bound for Calhoun Falls
swerved into a roadside ditch
to miss the truck coming head-on
grim and swift and in his lane
a wraith belonging to the death angel
riding like an ornament on its hood
and wearing the malevolent grin
of a mocking gargoyle.

In that short leap from the road
complete with a deceptive sensation
of hanging weightless in midair
it flew from the passing truck
on great, opaque wings, full-spread
to perch on the silver light mount
of the airborne patrol car
just before it dove into the ground
driving the left front chassis
like a free-spinning roulette wheel
into the seat on the driver's side
snaring the trooper in buckling steel
and erupting in a sheet of flames.

It sat outside and above the blaze
that crackled along the vinyl seats
and licked starch from the uniform
squatting there like a vulture would
while smoke boiled from the openings
and heat seared the pinned trooper
who sucked in its white-hot breath
as the bullets in his belt cooked off.

It would have waited without pity
for the flames to do their work
and draw the life from him
had that course not been interrupted
by someone passing by who stopped
and finally pried him loose.

It left through the gray billows
rising from the scorched grass
on wings large and lumbering
foiled and cheated for a time
and having lost the element of surprise
while he lived to make a full report
and give the detailed account
that sparked an all points bulletin.
There was time in the days remaining
to smile and say the hard goodbyes
and forge new steel for the spines
of those who stand a little straighter
when one respected from their ranks
falls in the line of duty.

In the Line of Duty: At 9 a.m. on May 6, 1959, State Highway
Patrolman Clyde Yonce swerved to avoid an oncoming truck while
en route to Calhoun Falls, South Carolina, from Abbeville on
Highway 72. His car burst into flames on impact after striking a
ditch to avoid a collision. Though Yonce was trapped in his 1957
Chevrolet patrol car, he was yanked free by the occupants of a passing
truck. Badly burned, he died thirteen days later from his injuries.
The truck that caused the accident, along with the vehicle it was
passing, were never identified nor their occupants apprehended.
Yonce, age 43, left a wife and two daughters ages sixteen and eleven.

Armadillos

With its kind probing the quadrants
and expanding like the universe
one made it out of the pine barrens
as far north as Eatonton
only to lie dead in the road
its body armor cracked open
and its carcass swollen double
a grim, surreal reminder that
there is no dignity in the death
of so small and squat a warrior.

The one they caught in Montrose
back in the late nineteen-fifties
caused people who never gathered
to come out of silent houses
to peek in a writhing sack
and when two grim men looked in
to gaze upon its defiance
they began to laugh like children
and then we knew it had the power
to create its own reality.

The lithe deer, the smart fox
the hound that reads the scent
enjoy the circuits made for them
while this one moves across them all
a bold, pint-sized conquistador
at war with every variable
plunging on to claim new lands
and following its own odd destiny
by the light of oncoming twin moons
and into the valley of the shadow.

Pissin' Rock

It was one of those bad years
at home as well as overseas
though it was never fully registered
until that last night out on recon
sweat-soaked and steamy
and in jungle rot up to one's crotch
when his buddies out in front
momentarily forgot themselves
in a dense cloud of mosquitoes
and accidently tripped a wire
causing them to fall and writhe
like huge dolls in camouflage
with their batteries winding down
and those unscathed to limp back
toting their sagging fetid forms
like shifting sacks of salt
blood souring on wet straining backs
as trauma and adrenaline plunged them
backward in a childish flight
to some grim Halloween evening
carried much too far.

He had grieved his father's death
while working through the layer of grease
in a ration can of limas
and squatting in a sweltering poncho
waiting for the rain to stop
and he had coped with the betrayal
that came in the brief Dear John
sitting in the doorway of a chopper
on its way to pick up bodies
in a Godforsaken sector where

a firebase had been overrun
but there was a hellish bedlam
straining from the depths of him
like gears grinding in their locks
and on that final bloody night
it went off like a starburst
when he came in hollow-eyed and found
another letter gloating on the bunk
with news about his sister running off
to join a commune and become
another casualty of war.

It was an extremely bad year
and though it rounded out his tour
and got him a Distinguished Service Medal
it took another five back home
to get a handle on the nervous tics
and twitches that would wrack his frame
each time he'd have those flashbacks
but it wasn't the prescription drugs
or those long psychiatric sessions
as an outpatient at the V.A.
that worked to bring him back around.
It was the melting shame he felt
for cracking from the mounting strain
when he had modeled pride and valor
and proved it under fire;
a shame that stung his cheeks
when he was spat upon in airports
and jeered in parking lots;
it was the rotten low-down dirty
stabbing bite of shame that saved him!
That --and the rock he found.

He rolled it uphill from the creek
through the woods behind the house
and set it up like a totem
in one far corner of the yard
then bought a can of red spray paint
to emblazon it on the side
with numbers one-nine-six-eight
to memorialize that bad year
and every time the tic came back
and brought that burning shame
he'd go outside and christen it
or get up in the night and christen it
and find the twitching would subside.
Such therapeutic measures served until
a female rural carrier drove the route
and spied his desecration from the road
and dialed the law up twice about it
but found to her profound disgust
the polite but official reply to be
that you just couldn't fault a man
for working on his sanity.

Broken Covey

Pulling out two smoking shells
from the Stevens twelve gauge
after catching them on the rise
and killing two and winging one
he watched the others scatter
like shot across the field
while thinking about his mother
old and spent and still grieving
the loss of both her parents
that year of the influenza
and the farming out of children
to different distant relatives.
One wrote her from Missouri
a year before he died
remembering her as a little girl
tear-stained and waving
in front of a Georgia depot
as she was spirited away
but she never found the rest.
It led the conversation
at many late supper tables
as she fed her own brood
this story of her family
often ladling it to him
in generous second helpings
creating guilt for his sins
however slight or incidental
against the smaller ones.
Thumbing in two fresh shells
before closing the breech
he wondered at age sixty-three
why it had crossed his mind
as he whistled to the dog
and moved out to search
for singles.

Iris

Among the first to unfurl flags
their stint is all too brief
yet for a time they stand erect
like guards at the yard borders
their green spears sharp and bristling
beneath the Bedouin headdresses
that billow as they wait in line
ready to be broached and overwhelmed
by an onslaught of seasonal color
bursting forth from all directions
until their glory fades from view
and they lie brown-tipped and spent
as though beaten back by hordes
into their mass of crab-like roots
to mend themselves and wait in caves
for the next trumpet.

When Cotton was King

On one of those soft days in June
just shy of his twenty-second birthday
when everyone his age was seeking work
through the National Youth Administration
he applied by mail and got the job
which came with an orange certificate
from the Department of Agriculture
and sixty-six feet of rolled chain
fed from the craw of a metal frame
to plot each green, leafing field
and determine the cotton allotment
its length glinting like a silver snake
on its way through the fringe grasses.

The first crops checked held overage
double-checked by hand the same afternoon
before measuring it with a planimeter
against aerial photos of the previous year
spread across the county agent's table
like maps from an ashen planet
yet singular enough in their detail
to find the Gaines farm noncompliant
with twenty-three acres under cultivation
that should have lain there fallow
bringing to pass an old-fashioned war
that pitted every high ideal of youth
against the meanness spawned by age.

"You will have to plow it under,"
he said to the likes of Ira Gaines
who shifted the tobacco cud about
as he gripped the porch rail hard

and said, "I'm damned if that's so!"
then ducked into the darkened house
and returned with a loaded shotgun
which he raised without another word
and fired into the young man's chest
its impact flinging him straight back
into the trunk of the shade tree
with roots extended like old claws
hard and clutching, never letting go.

Terrapin Shell

When he kicked it up in oak leaves
on the last day of deer season
amazed by how white it was
and how it slid into his coat pocket
cool and smooth to the touch
and ridged like a baby's skull
he knew he'd find a use for it.

Later while seated on a log
finishing off the dry lunch
of boiled eggs and fried sidemeat
he pulled it out and turned it
figuring it for an ashtray
then ran his fingers on the inside
up and down the bone-like ribs.

There in the deep quiet
dank with the smell of centuries
he studied the delicate curve
of arches anchored on their piers
at intervals around the flared lip
and suddenly he was back there
trooping into Rome with the Fifth

Wide-eyed in awe at age nineteen
and gawking alongside two others
who were part of the brown line
that had struggled up the Boot
gazing upward for the longest
at the ribs of a cathedral dome
mesmerized by its angular grace.

A limb breaking high somewhere
snatched him in its suddenness
from images of youth and war
to the steel of hard realities
where he surmised the truth
like a burst from a Very pistol
streaking across green-lit night.

That which left the mind of man
to cast its patterns and designs
upon Europe's vaulted ceilings
first crawled upon the ground
which was why he stooped down
and placed it once more in leaves
and out of reverence left it there.

Honest Flaw

While Walter worked the produce bins
at the *Southside Stop and Save*
rubbing dull cucumbers to a sheen
with dabs of harmless wax
and freshening celery and cabbages
with perpetual jets of spray
he watched selecting hands and eyes
of those who would play God
among the blemishes and dents
as if they alone reserved the right
to harshly judge the honest flaw.
There was Maidie whose cough drops
could not surpress her telling breath
and Rita whose ever-widening waist
no longer hid her dressed-up sin
and Oscar, unshorn and unbathed,
who pawed and picked over the fruit
while letting out a string of curses
but found no spots that could equal
the dried stains on his pants.
As he removed a blackened banana
no longer viable in the bunch
and picked up a bruised apple
that Oscar had taken his text upon
Walter took one of his own
and, as Lord of this garden,
polished its attractive side
and placed it back on the heap
and whispered, "Be ye perfect."

More Crate Talk

Webb was swatting the blowflies
in the corners of the plate glass
just back of the cash register
when the rest got back from Bab's
where they had grabbed a bite.
It was silence for the longest
until he finally put the swatter down
and began to speak his mind
after opening up a sweet drink
and a pack of headache powders:

"Feller came in the station
while you boys was gone
asking directions to Bellville. . .
said he was as lost as a branch rabbit.
That's one I ain't heard before."

Then Ed said,
"I was a boy nearly grown
when they got around to clearing off
those old brushpiles on the Milford place.
They set fire to them first
and ran all the rabbits out.
Them that weren't killed were confused. . .
easy pickings with a broom handle
like rats over at the dump.
When I hear somebody say
they're lost as a branch rabbit
I think about that place.
God, that fire was hot."

Then Spec said,
"They never did find that little Talmadge girl. . .
wandered off when her mama wasn't looking.
I always said she wasn't right!
I went out there with the rest of them . . .
helped them look about three days
but she never turned up.
Nobody could figure it out
unless she fell in the river
and she could have.
People ought to have better sense
than to let an afflicted child
just walk away like that."

Then Bob said,
"Speaking of no sense. . .
You remember Oscar Shaw. . .
been dead about twelve years now.
Always getting lost.
Never would stop and ask directions. . .
too proud or just too plain lazy
to get out and go to the trouble.
He was on his way once
to a revival at Smyrna
with a car full of old women
from that church they all go to
over at the Crossroads
and got all turned around. . .
all of them old women advising him
on which way to turn.
The meeting was over by the time
 he pulled up in the church yard.
Those old women were fuming, too.
Oscar never gave 'em an apology
or even let on that he felt bad about it.
He just walked up the front steps
as church was letting out and said,

'Preacher, you might not believe it
but there is a world of land
between here and home.'"

Webb rounded it out:
"I recall those two old boys from Crafton
On up in their eighties. . .
that'd be Junior Bateman and Cleeb
too old to do anything but sit
but I guess they got tired of it.
They took a notion one evening
to go to the wrestling matches in Macon.
Never been to one in their life
but watched it on the television for years
like Friday night religion. . .
had a favorite one called Avenger
with hair like a nest of red wasps. . .
anyhow he was down to come to Macon
and they drove themselves over there. . .
had a big time, too
but they got lost coming home. . .
all them bright lights hittin' 'em
late at night like that. . .
Gracie Massengale knows them . . .
says they got to talking
and went the wrong way on I-16
and wound up in Jacksonville, Florida . . .
said it took them three days
yakking and rambling backroads
to finally get back home."

Then he said,
"That cross-eyed Hammond kid
in here all the time with a yo-yo
stopped by and said he's getting married.
God help him, he's pitiful . . .
guess he'll wish he was lost
about a month from now."

Bereft

The mockingbirds have been uprooted
their sharp-tipped, impenetrable shrubbery
jerked from the ground by tractors
belching heavy-scented plumes
and straining on rusted chains.

More room will be made here
on the hospital's aging side
for those taken by the same surprise
whose time will suddenly come
to give up and give way.

Just as the birds return here
to light and chirp on the bare spots
they will dream of going back
to the closed house where dust
accumulates on all their things.

Gypsy's Curse

They would have taken the baby
had it not been for Maidie Pate
who watched them leave the cooking fire
to peek in the white wicker bassinet
placed in the shade of the side porch
and then lapse into their gibberish
and dart their black eyes about
to see if anyone was watching
smiling through a thin veneer
of feigned and fickle compliments
that hid designs more sinister.

Irv had agreed to let them camp
by the white rocks in the lane
between the house and store building
and get their water from the spigot
dripping right outside the store
assuming they would keep to themselves
in the vicinity of the curtained wagon
grateful for the afforded privilege
and not go milling about his place
or hanging around his storefront
unless they wanted to buy something.

He was in the back storeroom
busy with Maidie's feed sacks
and her mouth going a mile a minute
remarking on the colors of the prints
when she looked out toward the house
and noticed those kerchiefed heads
nodding in the direction of the bassinet
and warned Irv about roving gypsies

and their affinity for stealing children
right out from under the noses
of unsuspecting folks like him.

Not one to trifle with a thing
Irv ran them out of the yard
before they got their supper cooked
turning a deaf ear to the protests
falling like hail from the wagon
which were mainly in a foreign tongue.
When they were a ways down the road
the old man in the group looked back
and yelled something and made gestures
which Irv never could figure out
until his store burned that next April.

Sinking Spell

Blanche had hers on the front porch
in one of those enameled metal chairs
that had some spring to it.
She was minding her oldest grandchild
rocking back and forth in the porch swing
and that motion added to her own
got the upper end of things
causing her to slide from the chair
like a pebble from a hill
where the earth has given way.

In the brief time that elapsed
before Martha Joyce yelled out, "Mama!"
through a mouthful of clothespins
Blanche was spirited far away
to that spring day in 1908
when she rode upon the plowstock
brown curls tumbling before her
casting their shadow on the ground
as she balanced on the beam
with mirth pouring from her throat.

When her father's calloused hand
brown from the sun and big-veined
came from the long-sleeved khaki shirt
to steady and support, she knew
she never wanted to come back
though a voice from a dark well
kept repeating the word, "Mama!"
until she shot to the surface
and looked into her daughter's face
with unmistakable resentment.

Silver Bullet

From the size of the paw print
that would fill a man's palm
it had to be a large cat
like the one he got a glimpse of
when it cleaned out his chicken pen
and his old blue-tick hound
alongside Sam Cann's border collie
chased it clear out of hearing
though neither one came back.
That was when he knew that something
with movements swift and chilling
not driven by fright or hunger
was killing for the love of it.

The last of his five scrub cows
lay sprawled and stiff in death
the base of its throat chewed out
and wide claw-rakes slashed deep
in the thin meat of the shoulders.
It had been so with the others
throats torn out and drained dry
and gaunt carcasses left untouched
as if it meant to ruin him
by destroying them one by one
their lives being but the means
through which its shadow could slink
and steal his substance from him.

He had shot at its floating form
a month after he lost the dog
when it pulled down the only calf

moving like a phantom in the woods
indistinguishable in the starlit dawn
from the rustling of wind-stirred leaves
and he had fired in its direction
the night it appeared among his hogs
to litter his fields with carnage
and on one other rain-soaked evening
when it took all the white geese
that were nesting by the pond
but his shots never came close.

All that remained was the mule
old and gray and swaybacked
and hardly a loss worth crying over
even if it died like the others
yet one he could ill-afford
to just sit by and let happen.
The thing had been impossible to kill
evoking thoughts of an evil presence
more sinister than just a beast
bent on satisfying its blood lust
on an arthritic stable mule
but he knew it would come for it
and that called for stronger measures.

It took longer than he had expected
to melt the gleaming silver from
a nineteen-twenty-four Liberty dollar
but he pressed it in the mold
and crimped it in the casing
with the same amount of powder grains
that came in store-bought ammunition
then took a rocker from the porch
and a wool blanket to wrap in
and settled down to spend each night
in a shaded portion of the yard
within easy range of the barn loft
and its single, solitary opening.

He sat dew-beaded for nights on end
keeping a cold and sleepless vigil
like a soldier on the eve of battle
never losing the edge of wariness
yet amazed by the subtle reacquaintances
with old and familiar night sounds
complete with their childhood twinges.
He had drifted dead away like that
when a screech chilled his marrow
and a brown blur bounded by him
before he could even raise the gun
leaving him with a pounding heart
and the kicks of a dying mule.

He kept to his spot in the yard
even on the nights he got rain-drenched
knowing it would come back to gloat
or attempt to put its fangs in him.
This was no ordinary killer beast
marking the limits of its territory
but a presence stalking the world
with its black heart fixed on him
so singular in its unerring will
that he would catch sleep in the day
to avoid being bleary-eyed each night
becoming as nocturnal as the beast
and forging a savage kinship with it.

The long months of heat and cold
were taking a mounting toll on him
while constellations shifted overhead
their circuits bearing them ever westward
as he languished there and wondered
if the bullet in its brass casing
had not tarnished in the gun.
July went the way of May and June
and still no fresh sign or sighting
only a whispering from the broom sage

111

that had claimed his idle fields
like a knife blade stroking a strap
each evening before the wind laid.

After an endless string of humid nights
rank with the odor of souring peas
that were mowed but not turned over
he saw it coming from a distance
just as a sultry day was breaking
and an orange tint bathed its mottled coat.
It crossed from the sage to the pea patch
knowing full well he was sitting there
but never pausing in its liquid steps
coming to him like an obedient pet
to eventually stop at the yard's edge
and sit down on its haunches
licking a forepaw as it waited.

The moment paused there frozen
like a wingbeat caught on film
as neither of them moved a hair
but just sat still for the longest
looking into each other's eyes
to view things held in common
without malice and without fear.
While it held him in its yellow gaze
he thought about the months he'd spent
learning how to live with it
communing and commingling with it
at home with its malevolence
and hating for it to end like this.

He shot it as it sat there
the bullet driven like a cold hammer
through the skull above the eyes
its power forcing him from the chair
to stand hunched and straddle-legged
when it rocked him back forward

his eyes never leaving its sightless ones
as it stretched out before him
like a house cat going to sleep
its relaxed and graceful movement
prompting him to go and stand over it
where he felt small under the sky
and overwhelmed by a great loneliness.

Imposition

Have you ever wondered
what happens to a trimming
when it is clipped from the nail
to fall outside in grass?
Does some insect bear it home
like a hunter toting ivory
and is there proper recognition
for this prized trophy
and celebrations of the find
as songs around our campfires?
Perhaps on planes more singular
there is only habitual gathering
of what falls from the sky
and no great wonderment.

West Hell

You know how hot it's been!
It's so hot in the westside projects
nobody can stand to stay inside
and it's too hot on the porch slabs
to sit down on that slick cement.
It'll burn right through your clothes
and raise a blister on the skin
if a bare leg touches it.

Nothing to do all day long
but stand around and swelter
and watch old Pet mop her face
and shell her pan of peas.
Nobody else is out on this end
except her oldest named Darnel
wet shirt sticking to his back
leaning and shrugging and sulking
and stomping out his cigarettes
out of work and short on money.
She'll get up in a little while
and put five dollars in the mail
for a preacher on the television
and he'll just stand right there
and smoke and watch her do it
and when she goes back in
to set those peas to boiling
he will walk out to the road
and steal her money from the box

and twist it right out of the envelope
with one of those skinny hairpins.

Nobody on the other end but Shug
and he ain't never been right
sits all day in that wool cap
no matter how hot it's been
and watches the roaches crawl
and listens to the babies cry
while cars bubble on the road
back and forth, honk and wave.
He'll get up in a little while
and go three doors down then left
and three more to his sister's place
where he'll jimmy the back lock
to get in and look around
with them off at work or school.
He's never taken anything
but this time before he leaves
he plans on finding the baby doll
belonging to his sister's child
and because there's nothing else to do
he'll probably cut its hair.

At three o'clock in the afternoon
when the sun beats down the hottest
and the leaves begin to wither
an old man will walk the road
in a suit all shining black
and if he sees you watching him
he'll point a cane and hex you.
Folks let him pass like death
saying that he's really the Devil
out there checking on his dominion

to stoke things just a little hotter
and even Pet and Shug go in
though Darnel just stands and stares
like he's daring the old man to stop
and point that cane at him
thinking nothing will come of it
but he can't judge the Devil's work.
He's liable to keel right over
while he's standing there smirking
with the sun bearing down on him
or smother in the dead of night
when there's nothing to stir the air.
You know how hot it's been!

Keiser's Pigeons

We never knew why they belonged here
or dreamed their mingling generations
could go back that far
but they wrote the town's signature
in droppings from the early power lines
until they became a nuisance
and were shot off the gabled houses
and the window sills of the mill
especially after little Jimmy Proctor died
from breathing their filth into his lungs
while feeding the ones he tamed.
Their foul, pellet-filled nests
were cleared from clapboard boxing
and the brick niches in the smokestack
but it only thinned their ranks.
Just like the virile offspring
of those who paved the roads
and ginned the burlapped bales
and left to fight the wars
they have come back each time
to club in greater numbers
and to roost on the water tower
and accentuate the town's skyline
with their bold, persistent flocks
as much at home above these streets
as the rest of us below.

Keiser's Pigeons: Ed Keiser, a German immigrant who had once worked for James Edward Calhoun, was an early merchant at Calhoun Falls, S.C. He had married a mulatto woman, though the state of South Carolina did not recognize interracial marriages at the time. On the night of December 29, 1926, when he had become elderly, he was murdered by a black employee. Keiser had a pigeon loft which was probably abandoned at his death. The pigeons remained in the area and thrived on their own. Many persons contending with them over the years were never aware of their origin. See: Ernest M. Lander, Jr. *Tales of Calhoun Falls.* pp. 11, 47.

In the Eye of Peril

It called for twelve stitches
running up the right forearm
where he had shielded himself
from the swift but errant blade
of one of those old hawksbill knives
that would have found his heart
or an artery near the throat
had the preacher not stepped in
and let the point snag his Bible
on its second rake-through
ripping through most of Genesis
and finally hanging there
as things quieted back down.

He'd gone to their night meeting
down near the railroad tracks
at the edge of the village houses
on the mill's better side
and was seated on the second row
when a woman in the choir
kept cutting her eyes his way
about midway through the sermon
provoking an eventual smile from him
that caused her face to burn
which was not lost on her husband
a fixer on the second shift
enjoying his only evening off.

The preacher saw it coming
and hopped over the altar rail
just in time to raise his book

a large and limber rendition
of the red-lettered King James
to catch the intended death blow
his tongue sharp and on fire
about how it was a house of prayer
and not the devil's meeting place
calling for all the men to stand
and for the door to be blocked
as he prayed and sweated
laboring against the power of sin.

Grown men came close to crying
pressed there in each other's grip
while the women sobbed and shouted
and the Spirit grieved and groaned
for every ardent soul to be reborn.
Husband and wife were both reclaimed
praying on each other's neck
then reaching out to touch the arm
and soothe the still-bleeding visitor
who was hugged by his assailant
and remained joined at the hip with him
until forgiveness ended its work
and the mill whistle blew midnight.

No Man's Land

If you eat that white, fried side meat
it'll put demons in your blood
like it did for old grudge-bearing Hudson
and that mean, gun-toting Parnell
whose argument over the property line
was split down the middle of a road
where each claimed the opposite side.

Long after the conversation had played out
with neither giving an inch of road
Hudson took his old International Harvester
and plowed its width and length
planting the space in bush beans
which Parnell pulled up, one by one,
and laid beside the holes.

That fall Parnell fenced the road
driving the locust posts on Hudson's side
and tacking on three strands of wire
which lay in neat, twelve inch pieces
in the dawn of the next morning
where Hudson had snipped it off
ruining it for any future use.

The feud continued back and forth
until both grew old and died
their children selling the land off
before the grave dirt settled
to the Little River Hunting Club
whose members still tramp and stalk
where kudzu hides a multitude of sins.

Mowing Fields

From sunup to an early dusk
in the high meadow and the lush bottoms
many's the creature that by day
goes down to death in the mowing fields
pinched between close leathery stalks
or sliced and diced by the silver blade
or ground under a hard rubber tire
and left to swim or drown in pooling dew
grasshoppers moving sideways on one leg
crickets moping, cut in half
and dragging pieces of themselves along
sleeping fireflies by the thousands
with their wings tucked in prayer
luckless toads trapped in a labyrinth
spared but waiting for the next swift pass
alongside spent moths and lowly ticks
and skippers under every green spear
and spiders toting sacks of eggs
cutworms and inchworms and larvae
wrapped in their tight-spun coffins
and snails leaving their diamond trails
all marked unwittingly for sacrifice
by those who plant and prosper
who rake and claw and cultivate
to make the Earth a better place
and who are led in all their doings
by a Word deemed pure and holy
that sends them into beds and fields
to bring forth fruit and multiply
and to claim and name each creature
oblivious to its world of pain.

Midnight Grill

Moe had just wiped things clean
when a stranger came inside
surveying the vacant booths
and the one tight and teen-packed
in a far back corner by the box
before slipping onto a counter stool
to order coffee, strong and black.

He was no ordinary soul
in the long-tailed white tuxedo
with a pink shirt open at the neck
a lighted cigarette in one hand
folded city paper in the other
and hair well-oiled, brushed back
and shining like a raven's wing.

The corner table came alive
as patrons recognized the face
and huddled in a human lump
to pit their thoughts together
in a pile of grunts and whispers
then stared with awe and disbelief.
"Ain't that Daluka? Ain't that him?"

One of them rose in deference
and punched E Seven on the box
watching the spin and selection
and then the unerring needle drop
to play "The Last Goodbye"
the latest hit by Johnny Daluka
and his famous Solitaires.

Recognizing the lead-in instantly
he looked up and flashed a smile
then went back to his paper
never once lifting to his lips
the hand that held the cigarette
or picking up the steaming cup
to taste its bitter brew.

He left on the third play
while they mustered up the nerve
then rushed right out behind him
to stand in the empty drive
devoid of light or sound
where a dull ribbon of highway
stretched off into the night.

The crisp, late-night edition
left beside the untouched mug
was folded open to page three
sprouting a small headline that read:
"Plane lost off Florida Keys
Johnny Daluka and Band feared dead!
No wreckage! No survivors!"

Reminders

All the iron men have rusted
their women worn down like shovels
and their time like the rubble heaps
of old chimneyed house places.
They have left no blood heirs
to stride in their shadows
and replenish their deeds
or minstrels to praise their days
only broken pipe racks
and corroded Zippo lighters
and tarnished shaving kits
decorating forgotten bottom drawers
like mottled relics in a tomb
each one quoting a separate page
from these sagas of the dead.

Bedpan Commando

He came to work that first night
in sneakers and a sea-green smock
hands sweating under latex gloves
and possessing the hero visage
seen on that hospital tv show
while being caught up in the glamor
afforded those whose honed skills
gain them sanction and permission
to preside over life and death
with undisputed claim and privilege.

Such dotings were soon left behind
in the noise of barked commands
and in the endless miles of corridors
colliding with other milling orderlies
pushing buggies of hazardous waste
and in the spills of blood and filth
befitting those of his low station
and the great numbing shocks
that came from placing catheters
in the old and fat and misshapen.

At the end of a nightmare week
besieged by sights and smells
alien to the wildest imagination
he slipped into a supply closet
while being paged over the intercom
to give an enema in two-fourteen
and hid behind a towel rack
resolved to wait for the shift change
and count the dragging minutes
until he bowed to guilt and went.

Too traumatized to enumerate
indecencies which defied description
and sights that bordered on disbelief
he emerged in noxious clothes
soiled and besmirched and reeking
and went back to that dark closet
like a dog returning to its vomit
to repent all grandiosity and pride
and bewail all manifold fantasies
and to pray for God to call him home.

Haunts

Revisiting all the places
where life has come and gone
and those once known have died
seeing how the earth has moved
and the night sky has shifted
and the rivers have dried
proves that the best of times
slip gently from the bough
like dreams going unremembered
to lodge among the old foundations
cold and unrepentant.

Ambience

I remember Grandmother
magazine-fresh and smiling
with a look of ageless grace
that almost made one think
she had stepped from the cover
of the *Ladies Home Journal*
to stand among her zinnias
bending as a princess would
to smell the lavenders and pinks
and fondle each silken head
turned down in shameless pouting
like spoiled and resistant children
bored by her constant doting.

Into this bright garden realm
I longed to walk with her
on the cloudless sapphire days
toes touching dampened earth
beneath aromatic sun-turned stalks
until the day she gave me
my favorite butterflies encased
behind a pane of glass
pressed flat enough to count
each dot on the Buckeye
and trace the delicate embroidery
on the Monarch and the Swallowtail.

With my slim hand in hers
we entered the dark sanctum
of the closed-off guest bedroom
where frantic wings beat hard
against the smooth and rounded sides
of a tightly sealed Mason jar
as thin gossamer creatures
choked by the pungent mothballs
careened like stringless kites.
One by one, I saw them die
then watched them pinned to dry
before running back outside
wishing to forget her smile.

Consolation

Drinking beer down at the Little Tee-Pee
and punching in those suffer songs
was doing wonders for his disposition
until somebody lit up the pinball machine
and rang bells all through a wet one
being sung by Patsy Cline.
Going forth to protest his displeasure
he tripped and fell upon the Philistine
hunched with his thumbs on the flippers
breaking a quarter's worth of concentration
on its way to top a hundred thousand
for the first time in recent memory
and paying for it the hard way.

The next thing he remembered
was being helped up from the floor
mouth swollen and head throbbing
like he had been hit with a blivet.
Back on the stool at the bar
gazing at the dregs of dirty suds
drying near the bottom of the glass
and once more marinating in misery
his mind went ahead of his fingers
in a series of unrehearsed movements
all the way to the loaded shotgun
collecting dust behind the bar.

He could see himself holding it
with both barrels trained and ready
while the giant groveled on the floor
apologizing and begging for his life.
What happened next would be his call

and he'd be tempted to cut loose.
But, naw! He guess he'd let him live
remembering how his mother always said
that in him beat a heart of gold.
With that vivid recollection of himself
looking back from the empty glass
he dismissed the nourished grievance
and, rising with an air of benevolence,
paid the tab and left the bar.

Witch's Tit

The empty stare of house and lot
concealed in thick deepening shade
that reached like black-gloved fingers
out to a sparkling sunlit walk
was given wide and spacious berth
by boys in dread of hearing
the shrill after-school commands
of its ancient bow-backed crone
who scowled each time and warned us
at the threat of death or worse
to always keep away from there.

When I was asked to cut the yard
it took more than a dare
to enter the gloom and tangle
and gnaw around the crusting house
where old paint had dried and flaked
like gray and crumbling gingerbread
and fight the urge to gravitate
to the one bright backyard spot
under familiar Cold War skies
filled with their billowing contrails
from silver birds with trailing plumes.

As I filled the second tank
with faith prevailing over fear
and enough conviction welling up
to spit in the face of the wolf
she came out with a glass and said
she'd brought me something wet and cold.
I thanked her, smiled and almost bought
this change of withered heart until
I raised it to my lips and saw
a spider trapped between the cubes
and closed my eyes and drank.

I never cut her grass again
for reasons long expired with time
but held it by design or accident
to be up there with fights and threats
and brushes with one's finitude.
It hangs among the larger guilts
of Christ's betrayal with a kiss
and Caesar being shafted by his friend
and it will shout its loud reproofs
as sure as spiders crawl the wall
and as long as snakes go blind.

Options

There are never any good ones
for the fledgling from the nest
that gets pushed out too early
and lies bruised upon the ground
its frame unsightly and unformed
and its oversized yellow beak
open wide in grotesque bids
for food that will never come.

And there are no good ones
for the thin strip of a boy
skinned at the knees and elbows
who stumbles upon its world
and bends down close enough
to view its helpless plight
and feels compelled to intervene
once its tiny eye finds his.

He can take it in the house
to watch it shriek and die
or stand guard against the cat
and pray for a maternal rescue
he knows will not take place
or just walk off and leave --
each choice made a harbinger
of all that is forthcoming.

Clisbys

They both stood to inherit
once the *patron* of the family died
and he had it locked up so precise
that only the buzzards on the place
went unmentioned in his will of which
the twenty-odd pages guaranteed
codicil by codicil in aforesaids
the legal team earning its keep
and his own iron fist in things
from the rest home to the grave.

When he expired at ninety-three
it all went to his sole surviving child
a maid who never left the house
at one now with the rust and antiques
clinging to her like drag chains
and bitter from the curse of years
that found her nursing aging relatives
and gaining for her cares and pains
the run of house and farm lying situate
on three thousand acres of emptiness.

Only at her death was it to go
to the one remaining blood heir
and last of the Clisby line
a nephew who had made his mark
selling stocks for an Atlanta firm
and to whom she gave her blessing
to build a cabin in the woods
if he could spare from hunting trips
a little time to sit and talk
and celebrate the past a bit.

It did not take her long to find
the truth about these weekend trips
made like religious pilgrimages
by her nephew and his entourage
once the so-called lodge was built
and the raucous cries from wild parties
wafted on crisp winter evenings
straight into the cold of her bedroom
igniting a white rage in her flesh
that signified she'd had a bait of him.

And that's how she came to get
someone to drive her out there
on a day when the place stood vacant
and take the contents from each room
to be piled out in the yard like trash
and doused with gasoline and set ablaze
after spelling it out for the legal team
who sent him word by certified mail
never to set foot on the property
as long as she drew breath.

It rocked on that way for years
with no word to pass between them
while the lodge slowly melted away
in the saw briars and fox grapes
but on the day she died he came
and signed the otherwise blank paper
on the family side of the funeral register
without going in to view the body
or wasting a word on those attending
and with whom he'd gone to school.

The next day at the graveside
where friends stood in their Sunday best
he was elsewhere and in coveralls
astride a piece of heavy machinery
billowing its blue diesel smoke

and huffing like a winded beast
as he raised and lowered its blade
in the shade of her two yard oaks
sighting along the boxwood-lined walk
and then pointed it toward the house.

There being no slight interest or curiosity
in what she had kept untouched for him
or in the layered war of memories
stacked like old string-tied magazines
in the crevices of each upstairs closet
he struck the family pride full force
and bulldozed it into a deep gully
scraping and scooping far into the night
until not a trace of it remained
to vent a righteous spleen on him.

Just Dead Reckoning

Not by might nor power
says the scripture
but look here!
Not by rule nor square
has he made what is made.
From the backyard privy
to the tar-papered well house
he has sighted down the boards
and guided the saw with his thumb
down an imaginary line
and he has made what is made.
Do not defile it with measurements
of tape or string or plumb bob
it has been bred in him
like the bead work of spiders
or the inner gyroscopes of birds
winging their way south or north
into the distant vanishing points.
He will never lay the stones
by plans or specs or renderings
or pop a chalk line string
or read a bubble in a level
but his eye and heart are true
and his hand inclined
toward excellence.

Christmas Visit

Coming back in April for a funeral
after thirty years abstracted and away
he drove to all those places
waiting for him since childhood
and saw their ruin and desolation
reach out like hands to frisk him
and steal pieces of his heart.

No longer precious and intact
they smiled through the broken teeth
of hanging sash and banister
looking back at him from yard nettle
like pathetic elders grown feeble
smaller than he had remembered
with some sagging at the eaves.

The Sims house where he once played
had lost floor boards on its porch
and the Tyler place was overgrown
given over to owls and field mice
while farther down at the Barringtons
the spreading oaks had grayed into one
still serving as a buzzard's roost.

It was the same at the Templetons
and out on the Shinholster farm
with sprouts reclaiming the terraces
and old houses staring at the road
their abandonment and humiliation
exploding right before his eyes
like an unexpected covey of quail.

He left the South that evening
on a blinking red-eye from Atlanta
bound for the California coast

but flew back all those long miles
in the cold grip of late December
with decorations piled and pressed
in the trunk of a rental car.

At every house standing empty
he placed a wreath or a red bow
nailing it to a bolted door
or tying it around a post
until he had changed them all
from cheerless haunts to homes
that momentarily lived again.

He never came back South
but every year since that one
someone has changed the bows
and made the season brighter
for all who pass and recollect
that Christmas is about remembering
even those unnamed, unknown.

Gray Days

When the road is a silver ribbon
and a light fog haunts the trees
weeping openly at a distance
when all the animals lie nestled
or bunched in the shallow cavities
of the blond and barren fields
when there is reverence and softness
smelled in the pores of the earth
on its dank leaves and nettles
a crow will wing its way
dark and slow and solitary
like a mote in the mind's eye
and we will know our frame
forgetting who we have been
in the imagination of our hearts
and owning its brief passage
through the wet and clinging mists
as somehow closer to the truth
of where we are to go.

Old Friend

Looking at it sitting on the lot
dinked and dingy and antiquated
beside the newer graceful models
gleaming with a freshly lacquered sheen
it seemed to be the prudent thing
handing over the tag and title
and signing on the dotted line
and driving out of there in style
but the more he stared at it
the more inclined he was to sit
and turn into a pillar of salt.

Going back over those twelve years
of its bonding flesh with steel
it had been his willing instrument
responding in the worst of times
and traveling faithfully down the miles
like a mute but intimate companion
ferrying children into adolescent years
still bearing their scuffs and stains
but no longer reeking of hermit crab
found in the forgotten plastic bag
wedged in the crack of the back seat.

Clutching the new plastic-gripped keys
and sliding into soft molded contours
of the latest in performance and design
with its unfamiliar smells and features
he languished there like a kid
about to put his dog to sleep
fighting the urge to go back inside
and reclaim the abandoned trade-in
but as deceit dwells in all hearts
an unprecedented amount in his
changed gears and drove away

Polliwogs

Where is the wind when you need it?
This posed the singular question
for those mustered to the quarter deck
exuding the filth and stench of wharf rats
after sliding from the birth canal
of an endless, well-greased slop chute
staggering in the semblance of a line
formed to exercise the one-time privilege
of sucking the Royal Baby's toe
and being initiated by Neptunus Rex
into the sacred and solemn mysteries
of the ancient order of the deep.

Heads shaven and bowed in mock tribute
before this Ruler of the Raging Main
with their fates decided by the ship's lowly
and their vessel straddling where the zeroes
converge on the International Date Line
they qualify as trusted shellbacks
on this night when all officers and crew
dispense with the rules and regulations
having earned the right to be numbered
among those conducting future ceremonies
and to be acclaimed by their shipmates
as worthy seamen of the first water.

On an afternoon fifty years hence
while pulling old treasures from a drawer
to be viewed by fascinated grandchildren
one of them will unroll the tight scroll
of his colorful and inscribed certificate
with its abundance of lurid mermaids

riding dolphins at the four corners
and the old man with the devil's fork
breaking the waves on his white steeds
and will ask him to tell them what it means
and he will smile and answer this way,
"If I told you, you wouldn't understand!"

Polliwogs: Ceremonies held by the U.S. Navy while crossing the equator reached their zenith during World War II. Each "first-timer" underwent an initiation process that varied from ship to ship and received a certificate as a memento. Variations of this practice date to the 19th Century. In recent times, the U.S. Navy curtailed the activities of this "rite of passage" by imposing reasonable limits on what could be required of the novice being inducted.

Homebound

When Gaynelle fell that morning
attempting to stay ahead of the roach
frantic in its zig-zag haste to find
one of those out-of-the-way places
between the wall and double bed
she wedged there for the longest
straining and pulling against herself
with the intentions of a Prometheus
but the body of a spindly bird
finally breaking loose and dropping
as a large dam spewed and ruptured
in the hollow cleavage of her chest
then rolling under and out of sight
where she died tasting blood she thought
was dust from the bed springs.

The only one who checked was Sylvia
who saw the mail and daily papers
accumulate for three days running
and got her boy Donald to climb in
through an unlocked bathroom window
and let her in through the front.
After seeing nothing was amiss
they left satisfied she'd gone someplace
but just to make dead sure of it
a hurried call was placed to Edgar
the last of her local living kin
who spoke through an alcoholic fog
to say he had seen the pink forms
where she was to be taken to Alabama
and put in a nursing home.

Since Edgar had no number or address
there was nothing left to do but wait
though Sylvia prevailed upon her son
to cut off the water at the street
and take home the whining cat
while she stopped all the deliveries
and went back over that same week
without so much as peeping in the bedroom
to clean out and unplug the refrigerator
and take the few remaining items home
eventually calling the power people
to disconnect things at the pole
livid that Gaynelle would leave
and not have someone send her word.
She just probably forgot. Poor thing!

After two years of urging Edgar
to at least find out where to write
and hounding Donald to keep up the yard
Sylvia finally had the massive stroke
that was destined to take her out
all due to a little cornflake
breaking off in the left carotid
and traveling like flotsam to the brain
which put undue responsibilities on Donald
who completely let the other go
and absolved himself of the yard work
giving no more thought or consciousness
to the rusting of the window screens
or the peeling along the weatherboards
or the gray molting of the roof.

It was four years going on five
when Edgar stirred from his favorite chair
with the mercenary but charitable thought

of providing a better place to live
for one of his old soaked buddies
at an affordable price per month
but enough to gain back the tax
he'd paid out to keep Gaynelle's house
from falling too far in arrears
and him with no source of income
other than a little Social Security
and his monthly disabled veteran's check.
Surely it was fair to rent it out
to charge against what he had spent
to keep the title in her name.

There being no key with which to get in
he had to tap out a glass pane
just above the back door lock
but quickly came back outside.
God, there were roaches by the thousands
crawling on the walls and table tops.
You could hear them from the porch
buzzing and clicking their long antennae
like wasps worrying over a nest.
Their smell was something terrible
a noxious damp cellar odor
and it, more than anything else,
prompted an immediate and urgent call
to the first listing under pest control
and they could come that afternoon.

The panel truck pulled up on schedule
with little bug decals on the side
its driver popping gum and smiling
as he swiftly pumped the spray canister
and tested the nozzle on a tire
with a series of short toxic squirts.
Edgar told him he'd need a lot of it
to combat the legions he had seen

expressing doubts about getting them all
with just one pass through the house
and telling him to take his time
and be sure to get up under things
leaving him with this parting admonition:
"a body never knows what he'll find
looking under other people's beds."

Pallet Babies

Conceived in haste on rug or floor
because their progenitors could not wait
till evening's safe reclining hour
they are born under every star
and grow to be mere duplications
of the same unbridled passions
that filch the powers of self-control.
They are the arrogant and rude
who pout to have their way
or yell and curse their lungs out
at the slightest inconvenience
or the mildest irritation.
Never let them stir your blood
or cause you to acquiesce
to unbecoming and unrighteous thoughts.
Be merciful! Forgive them
and remember how they got here.

Mehetabel at High Tea

On the day she was able
to sit up and take nourishment
and cough out the great globs
of pneumonia in her lungs
a flushed and renewed Mehetabel
heady from an energetic burst
sat up in the high four-poster
and rang the bell for Delia
bent on hosting an occasion for
the society's remaining Daughters.

The next afternoon at three
when Delia wheeled her chair
across the heart-pine threshold
into the cool glossed parlor
the silver service was in place
as were the cups and saucers
on the little draped card tables
while the sideboard held the cream
and sugar cubes and iced tarts
ringing the mold of mint jelly.

In that far-reaching pause
before the first buzzer rang
she stared at the cut flowers
one to each bud vase
and saw their blush at once
like faces looking back
and heard their shrieks of pain.
The rose cried out to her,
"Look what you've done!"
The orchid said, "I'm dying!"
Even the fiery lily asked,
"Why have you severed me?"

151

After the guests settled for a chat
timing their benign compliments
to fit into prevailing moments
her mind could not shut out
the wails of floral anguish
heard above the words of friends.
She looked with widened eyes
and said, "I am a murderer!
All these years, I've been one!"
ending the polite conversations
and causing tea to spill
and strained smiles to break.

A fawning group arose as one
gushing out their flattery
and voicing great amazement
at how good she looked
and how gracious she had been
to decorate and entertain
so soon from the sickbed
asking her to have them back
and if they could get her recipe
before hurrying down the steps
to commiserate and then go tell
how badly she was slipping.

Sentinel

Under this canopy called heaven
where we will come to know
the end of everything we love
an angel weeps and watches
from a shedding grove.

Kathleen

Sometimes when she would pound her head
against the walls or the door frame
tapping out a code that signified distress
her parents never once deciphered it
as pleas from their drowning child
bobbing in a sea of mental illness
but locked her in a bedroom closet
as they divided between themselves
the feast of their great misgivings.

They sent her away to purge themselves
of all that it took to keep her
though she did not survive for long
as a little girl suddenly become
the prey of large and slobbering giants
dying gladly at the age of ten
having endured unspeakable humiliations
without word or visit from her family
in the long stretching of that single year.

When they brought her home to bury
how they all grieved and cried
and poured out rivers at the grave
but later into that care-worn evening
with the house unduly crowded
someone looked in a closet
and there for a brief unending moment
dressed in her black funeral clothes
sat the little girl looking back.

Twelfth Birthday

I never found the needle in the haystack
but I found the rabbit in the brush pile
working behind the sniffing bench-legged beagles
blowing frost and stomping limbs and clumps
until blood rushed in thin-veined folded ears
and one bolted from the warm and hard narrows
into the blinding glare of a frozen morning
amid the din of canine yelps and taunts
striking across red islands of spewed-up earth
into an endless sea of dead, ragged grasses
as the old butt-scarred Stevens .12-gauge
left the crook of a canvas-covered arm
and swung toward the birth of shouts and sounds
the faint smell of its oiled parts wafting
while an eye sighted down the grooved ridge
and caught the glint on the silver bead
and shifted it to that floating point
an inch or two beyond the rabbit's nose
before a finger found the left-hand trigger
and squeezed its cold curved moon of steel
sending a stinging jolt to the right shoulder
and death to the luckless, lightning hare
spilling end over end like a bowling pin
a scant breath ahead of the crying pack
its crimson sprinkled on their bristling coats.

Requiem

At his work station in Los Alamos
nearer than the hearts of men conceived
to the actual end of the Earth
it never fully registered with him
that he held within his infirm grasp
the power to recreate old worlds
or bend them to distorted shapes
in the touching of two smaller ones
fashioned and labeled U-235
to achieve the proper chain reaction.

During this one of numerous recipes
for bringing them to collision
and then prying their energies apart
before a fusion could be reached
the divider he was holding slipped
and the worlds blended and commingled
forcing him to quickly breach the shields
and separate them with his hands
just as the bluish aura leapt
to give a new and hellish birth.

While in that garish haze he saw
the atom split a thousand ways
and all the formulas for each
run end to end on electric current
flowing through his optic nerves
and right behind it the shorter burst
of human history in a lightning flash
and finally the head and gleaming eyes
of that creature raging just beyond us
complete with trunk and tusks.

Requiem: On May 21, 1946, Louis Slotin, a government researcher at Los Alamos, New Mexico, was conducting tests with uranium masses in an effort to determine the appropriate amount necessary to achieve critical mass. Having used a screwdriver to separate the material at the last moment in many experiments, on this occasion, the screwdriver slipped and the material began its process of fusion. Slotin separated it with his hands as the room filled with a dazzling bluish light, thus saving seven other people in the room but exposing himself to massive doses of radiation. He died nine days later from the exposure. This story may be found in George Vandeman's book, *Planet in Rebellion.*

Hoochie Mama

Sundown, pink sky, quiet street
standing out there, waitin' for a ride
leather skirt, string purse and high heels
don't look if you goin' home tonight
don't stop if you can't leave it all
she can take a man sittin' in church
and turn him into a gin-house fool
she makes him want to fight for her
she don't care what home she wreck
she a hoochie mama.

Bible says better to marry than burn
hoochie mama can make you burn
knows how to shake you out like a rag
and lead you like a Judas goat
straight down to the slaughter mill
smilin' at you all the way there
smilin' while they jug you with a knife
and be goin' with somebody else
while you laid out in the funeral parlor
she a hoochie mama.

There was this woman one time
she took a man's check on payday
meant to put bread on the table
and she go out and buy a talkin' bird
knowing she ain't gonna keep it
just playing while his wife and babies
sittin' there with nothing left to eat
don't let her get in your head
the honey ain't worth the killin' sting
she a . . . you know what she is!

Marasmus

Like the lone buzzard on its spiral
against the high-banked cloudy pillars
a rural pattern never varies on the hill
where felarks call for their own name's sake
across the wide expanse of pastured fields
and at two o'clock each Sunday afternoon
after having scraped and washed the plates
they take pleasure in the random gathering
of keys and coats and pocketbooks
and meet in the deep and shaded narrows
by frozen tractors in the side-shed
on ancient earth, gray and bug-drilled
and back out the pea-green Plymouth coupe
to tour the same worn country roads.

Little by little time has worn to nothing
like a favorite knife honed too thin
and the chicks in the yard have gone
and the chicks in the house have flown
and the man in the bed wastes away
his mind an ember among dead coals
his breath a faded word on the page
in a story that will eventually end
while she scrapes the last chipped plate
with its faded Blue Willow pattern
then dresses in those same Sunday clothes
leaving him locked inside the house
and goes out and sits awhile in that car
where years of grime coat the windshield.

Beggared Questions

What gave you a hardened eye?
Have you not seen color leap at you
time and again from the same gray bough
despite age and aches and attitudes
that ignore such joyous bursts of praise?
Have you not felt the sun come back
and reach in to nullify your bones
inviting you to shed like clothing
the drab and somber moods
and blush at what it stirs?
Have you not tasted on your lips
the transparent smears of pollen
brushing by on gossamer wings
that leave their crystalline sugar coating?
Who gave you the right to brood
so far into the dour despondent corners
that you have closed your eyes
to this emerging spectacle, this delicacy
which has once more arranged itself
like a table being spread before you
bidding you to cease and desist
from all the familiar deprivations
and let the child in you enjoy?

Trailer Trash

Unbeknownst to Monk Willis
low-life thieving son of Asher
there had been a killing in Texas
that claimed the life of Jace Rondel
the younger half-brother of Seab
who had been out there a week
all crossed up with the law
and having a devil of a time
navigating in that walk-in cooler
and straightening out the mix-up
having to do with the toe tags.
He had run short on cash and patience
by the time he finally cut a deal
with a man who ran a funeral home
and got Jace's last remains cremated
for less than the price it cost
to ship him back home in a box.
They gave him all that was Jace
in a little Zip-loc sandwich bag
and he drove straight through the night
eating his last handfull of pills
before pulling up in his own driveway
in the middle of the next night
long enough to get a change of clothes
and put that bag in a shoebox
that he slid under the bed
and then left for his sister, Jewellene's
who was waiting-up in Stockbridge.

Nothing got past Monk Willis
who had a pulse on all the action
going down under the lights each night
there in his daddy's trailer park

from dope smoking and pimping
to the occasional wife and child beatings
and the incessant rubber-laying
on that strip of frontage road
behind the row of double-wides.
He never missed a trick or beat
and that is how he came to be
lolled back in the layered shadows
flipping quarters in one hand
end over end with the thumb
when Seab wheeled in to his trailer
with nothing but that plastic bag
and eased back off without it
running on just his park lights.
He figured it for a drug deal
and his powers of deduction told him
that the stash was still inside
as he fingered the ring of duplicates
he'd borrowed from his daddy's desk
that bristled with shining spare keys
to every shed and trailer in the yard
giving things time to die down
and the night a chance to cool
before pulling off the perfect heist.

It was still and nudging four a.m.
when the right key fit the lock
and Monk, whose pupils had dilated
to the dime-size look of an owl,
felt his way around without a light
deft and expert in his pillaging
but in the dappled rays from cars
hitting the high beams as they came
off the curve on the frontage road
tense and bunched and as nervous
as a Chihuahua in a flea market.

After sniffing a ripe pair of dirty socks
crumpled in a wad by the doorway
and almost retching from the bile
that rose in the back of his throat
he cracked the refrigerator door enough
to distinguish objects otherwise unseen
then went in and located the prize
flexing his long arm under there
with all the wisdom of a snake
and lifting that bag out of the box.
In and out in ten minutes' time
he smirked from ear to ear
with an inflated sense of prowess
believing he had gotten his hands
on some quality stuff and confident
that he'd find a way to fence it
but aiming to smoke a little first.

The First Precept

We must graze the fields before us
in this great and wide complexity
while death in its relentlessness
nips at the flanks of the herd
positioning ourselves near the center
where there is some illusion of safety
though the air is stale and tight
and the fare has been browsed over.
We must not fail to stay alert
and poised for dangers unforeseen
lest we feel the rake of claws
that bring us to the grass
or the bite of fangs and know
the ripping of our own viscera.
It is not ours to see beyond
the limits that we shun and touch
in this ever-shifting migration --
only to run and wait!

Fishing on the Bottom

Just when all faith seemed lost
in the worn cogs of town government
the state grant money came through
and a new Caterpillar motor-grader
spray-painted the color of rat cheese
was trucked in from Raleigh-Durham
and deposited behind the chain-link
in the sand lot next to City Hall.

The dirt roads and back alleys
had run red in the spring rains
making garbage pick-up hit-and-miss
with the truck miring to the axles
about twelve to fifteen times a day
despite Chub Hulet hanging off the end
trying to spring for a little leverage
only to get encrusted for his pains.

The stench from weeks of pile-up
had cast a pall over the council members
and had taxpayers close to mutiny
when the long-awaited answer came
complete with blade-lift hydraulics
and a green digital display in the cab
that ran the Global Positioning System
and was a must for scraping roads.

The one hitch was someone qualified
in the operation of heavy equipment
and that always led to Delmer
usually fresh out of the tank
but ever eager to resurrect his skills
provided all his fines were paid
which the council voted to suspend
just to get him in the driver's seat.

He had not been at work a week
when the oil pan cracked and bled
and the gear box groaned and cried
and when told there'd be no fixing it
by the boys down at Dalrymple's garage
had it towed to the maintenance shed
where John Earle and Duck motioned him
to park it in a place out back.

It was deposited by the rusting hulks
of cement mixer cabs and broken tractors
bobcats, bulldozers and dump trucks
lined up like old destroyers in mothballs
that Delmer looked upon with pride
and said to Duck through misted eyes,
"In all my years working for the city
I drove every one of them."

Cicadas

When their sound was new to me
my own metamorphosis was a year old
and both were drowned by the roar
of the large olive-drab trucks
coming home from World War Two.
I grew while they were tunneling
erecting a thin shadow in the world
and when they boiled from the ground again
the music had changed and my heart
was fixed on a pair of white loafers.
I changed as they lay in the earth
and vanished when they came back out
to be one among the nameless city faces
far from their drone and humming.
In the next sleep, long and dreamless
I did not awake until the May morning
my children picked their skeletons off trees
and I marked well the mirth and innocence.
Now after thirteen misspent summers
they have emerged to whir and churr
and I have surveyed my erratic flight
while watching them soar and drop
new-winged but milling and helpless
telegraphing joy among themselves.

Shades of Pandora

No one opened a velvet-lined box
to loose its evil on the world
like moths springing from old closets
after fretting all the woolen garments
but it was nonetheless deliberate
as if nature's good and guiding hand
had raised itself to strike
all who dwelled beneath its shadow
and dwarf their warring carnage
with the visit of a pestilence
so great in its devastation
as to rival every ancient plague
and sow humility like crops of wheat
for grieving hearts to feed upon.

It made its advent in a bird
that left hard droppings by a fence
where a rooting sow nudged the wire
the week she went to market
her nervousness and wild skittishness
at being handled and displaced
causing it to unleash its proteins
and feed upon her weaknesses
there in the filthy crowded pens
growing and gaining full viral strength
by the time she was slaughtered
without pity by a butcher's son
the blood from her carcass splashing hot
against a fresh cut near the thumb.

He took it with him to the camp
signing the death warrants of millions
while filling out the induction papers
releasing it in airborne particles

that lodged with unsuspecting hosts
in the closed ranks on the drill field
and in the sweltering mess hall
each time he sneezed or coughed
shipping it by boatloads overseas
and by rail to towns and farms
to reap a great harvest of death
and cow the Earth for a time
with coffins full of evidence
about what still sleeps and waits.

Shades of Pandora: Researchers in 1997 have concluded that the 1918 influenza virus, which killed 21 million people in less than a year, originated at Camp Jackson, South Carolina, an induction center for soldiers leaving for France in WWI. The virus was transmitted to human beings from pigs, who normally contract it from birds, where it resides harmlessly. Reportedly, 700,000 persons died in the United States, including 43,000 servicemen.

Bless Its Little Heart

When babies fuss and fret and cry
pleading to be shushed and comforted
there are words with which to reach them
before they fathom sounds or languages
that work the charm of sweet repose
if said in the proper sequence
and with those critical inflections
carved only on the lost Rosettas
found in the hearts of grandmothers.
To miss them is uncivilizing
and casts upon the world in droves
lives that can never be consoled
by wealth or accolades or power
but that remain day after day
amongst great inherent miseries
for the purpose sole and singular
of striving and afflicting the peaceable
who were washed at least once
at this fountain of verbal bliss.

Better Off Dead

"Web Clifford's gone to his grave
and now Woodrow's gone to his!
I'll tell you what! They're better off!
They're better off than most of us!
You know they're bound to be!"
or so the conversation goes
out in the soft wood-grain rockers
on sultry nights, warm and light-tinged
with a ring of haze around the moon
sitting on the bannistered porch
lighted by the white yard floods
out at Dupree's Funeral Home
where graying heads in wide-brim hats
and old suits with wide lapels
exuding subtle mothball odors
recite the lot of fallen faded men
the large veins standing on their hands
as they pass the Prince Albert can
and spill leavings on the broken tile.

They have come to sit up awhile
to pass soft words and firm grips
and repeat the age-old homilies
to those who brace the widow's chair
abiding with unaccustomed toleration
the red-eyed teenage grandsons
of their befriended late departed
who sport earrings and ponytails
but they have ended on baser notes
at the dark end of the porch
moving from the latest medical opinion

on Herschel Rockdodger's flutter valve
on down to the crops and weather
before degenerating into knowing smirks
about someone's wife sneaking off
to meet a fellow out on a side road
only to have the law drive up and see her
with that got-caught look of a dog
trying to pass persimmon seeds.

Following this and other profane lapses
timed to offset the chill of death
creeping up their own starched collars
they gain the wherewithal to go inside
amid the soothing hums from hearing aids
heard over the recorded organ music
and stand around the rosebud casket spray
with its Styrofoam letters in golden glitter
spelling out the words, "God is love"
and shake each proffered hand again
as if to repeal everything obscene
while resurrecting worn-out stagnant lines
with power enough to comfort and uphold
the county-wide relations of the one
about to take the long dirt nap . . .
"You know you would not want him back
as sick and helpless as he was!
We'll miss him but he's better off!
You know he's 'bliged to be!"

Magi

Sometimes
the only Christmas worth having
comes worn and destitute and late
with a few waxed-wrapped pieces
of soft year-old fruitcake
and a warm swig of sherry
straight from the bottle
received like a sacrament
on a nameless stretch of road
in the sanctity of the car
where the taste bursts forth
like the birth of a new star
and smells waft into the soul
to rouse such overwhelming gratitude
there are newborn adorations
for old bearers of these gifts.

Bloody Buckets

There was a rough one called Chastain's
that used to sit across the road
from where they built the new school
run by a one-eyed, one-eared man
who packed a holstered meat cleaver
and another one named Devil's Den
where Obie Dixon was shot dead
down a red road by the river
below the city sewerage plant
and the boys from both of these
were real dirt-roller sports
who sometimes mixed it up in fights
but on occasion they piled in cars
to go across the county line
to one they called The Roost
tucked away in the cattails
where they would boast and strut
and recount their annihilations
before those too cowed and stupefied
to stand up and defend themselves
on knees as weak as water.

On one such moon-spent night
that struck the perfect brooder mood
the word of the bird preceded them
and when they braced The Roost
with sour breaths and knucks and chains
bent on smashing furniture and glass
and backing down the hard-line regulars
the brightness caused them all to squint
and find the lone emaciated man
sitting in the center of the room
wearing a pasted Bogart grin
and a hat brim shading hollow eyes
whom they recognized by lethal reputation

as someone called The Sleeper
a gassed veteran from the last war
with three fingers gone from one hand
and a bulge in his trench coat
that hid a Black Owl pocket pistol
propped back in his chair relaxed
and smiling like the familiar visage
on a can of Red Devil Lye.

As they ringed his solitary table
swelled with delusions of their might
yet drawn to that ashen face of his
which was seasoned like old lumber
The Sleeper rasped these words to them:
"You boys missed out on the main event!
So much blood was spilled last night
you couldn't wash it off the walls
or scrub the stains out of the floor
so I had'em paint it all in red
ceiling to floor! Welcome to hell!
Who wants the first dance?"
Those standing to his front were first
to read death in those eyes
and a chill shot straight through them
like someone walking on their grave
causing the knives and chains they brought
to rattle like loose pocket change
as they backed from the painted room
owning that as the first and only time
to turn and show the white feather.

Pretenders

In time the land will heal itself
sucking on old bricks and foundation stones
until they melt away under the grass
taking some of the broken pieces
of human legend with them

and in time the frogs will resound
with choruses in the dark and say:
"Who will now govern us?"
and all the lowly forms will answer
from the night: "Not I! Not I!"

and in time some being self-anointed
will arise and exclaim that it alone
was kissed by the lips of God
and given charge to rule the rest
and it will change the names again

and in time the scars it makes
will fade from sight and soul and mind
and the night voices once more will blend
to raise the loud reverberating question
until one of them hesitates, then comes.

Good to Go

On that last claustrophobic walk
down the yellow dim-lit corridor
undeniably headed for the chair
Bobby Lee didn't look so good
though he had a flash and wink
for grim, gray faces on the Row
who stayed up to see him off
and watch the lights flicker
and be thrilled with premonitions
of their own bleak prospects
while feeling a morbid satisfaction
over being hand-picked by fate
to stand there unmolested
and smell their own fear
once the switch was thrown.

Rounding the last sharp corner
with that large gray door in view
the subject blanched and balked
then swooned and swayed
losing the cool, calm demeanor
of a born serial killer
along with every shred of self-control
collapsing between two guards
who pinched him at the armpits
and angled themselves at an A-frame
so vomit would not hit their shoes
wondering how a heart so twisted
could lead a string of victims
to their deaths and not acquire
the stomach for his own.

The chaplain yelled out, "Bobby Lee!
Fix both your eyes on this!"
And he whipped out a paper fan

that bore the form of Jesus
complete with a bleeding heart
surrounded by a crown of thorns
and held it up before his face.
"Focus on Jesus, Bobby Lee!
He knows all about the dying time!
He's faced it, same as you!"
And pulling on the shirt front
with the haste of one about to be
too late to meet the Maker
he started down the polished hall
and said, "We're good to go!"

Good to Go: In Italy between the 14th and 17th centuries, persons about to be executed would be led to the block or gallows by members of a fraternal order who would hold before their faces a tavoletta. Resembling a large hand-held fan, these instruments of consolation would contain pictures on either side designed to empower the condemned individual. One side would be a scene from Christ's passion; on the other, a picture of a martyr. These images kept the victim spiritually focused and capable of completing the execution with dignity. See: David Freeberg. *The Power of Images: Studies in the History and Theory of Response.* Univ. of Chicago. pp. 5-9.

In Remembrance

More out of habit than hunger
he would get up in the dark
before squirrels scaled down the bark
or birds fussed about their territories
and roll out a pan of dough
making the biscuits like she did
never to rise over half an inch
as they swelled in the woodstove.

He lacked her swift and practiced grace
going from one burner to another
waiting for the grits to bubble
pouring coffee to cut the grease
as he stirred it into red-eye gravy
keeping close and nervous oversight
under a swaying sixty-watt bulb
in a kitchen pale as death.

He never ate that much of it
but would leave it there to cool
then scrape it out cold and clotted
and scatter it among the chickens.
Because there was little else to do
the whole house reeked of it
each time he would go and come
breathing in the smell of her.

Techniques

When it came to skinning rabbits
we used to pinch up the fur
right in the middle of its back
then slice down in the pinch and pull
so two of us could put fingers in
and shuck in opposite directions
leaving a thin strand on the belly
that was called the pucker string.
It was like taking the shirt and pants
off a little feller gone to sleep
but it left it free of hair
and ready to be opened up.

Then my grandpa had this uncle
who claimed he had a better way!
Said he learned it from an Indian
down in the Mississippi swamps
on what he called The Frogbone.
He'd just cut the head off first
and listen to the dogs crunch it
then lay hold of the hind legs
and sling the guts through the neck
getting them all over the dogs
and leaving the meat in the skin
until time came to cook it.

Said it was disrespectful to dogs
to take all the lust out of it
and let them gorge on everything at once
leaving the biggest to snarl and hog it
not to mention eating all that hair
off all those sore places

where the skin held a wolf.
Said you wouldn't eat it
but had no qualms at all
about feeding it to the dogs
which to his mind was a sin
and a ruination.

Techniques: The "wolf" in this mention refers to the larvae of the warble fly, a species of the botfly.

Counting Coup

He goes back at least once a year
and parks about midway in the long curve
where there used to be a peach orchard
and just stands on the side of the road
looking at a strand of rusted barbed wire
stapled to a post for more than fifty years.
Some of it still holds caught hair
from the time when the trees were cleared
and they ran cows of every description
in and out of the place in droves
until old man Swann bought the property
and let the briars and kudzu take it
but there is a place in that old fence
where the top wire sags so much
that it touches on the middle strand
and that's the spot he goes back to.

Not many people know the full story
and there's no way he would tell it now
but the day he came home from Korea
his brother was rushing to the station
when he flipped a car in that curve
and was pronounced dead at the scene.
It wasn't long after the car was moved
that he was visiting the same place
and a crow swooped down from nowhere
and brushed its wing on his left shoulder
but he didn't think any more about it
until he drove by there the next morning
and it touched its wing to his windshield
right in the middle of that curve
causing him to turn around and go back
where it dove on him a second time.

It went on like that for a year
each time he'd pass that particular place
and he'd own it to be no more
than just a wild thing having its fun
though it was an encouragement to him
having to travel that road every day
with the crow becoming a dark companion
that never failed to find his car.
He didn't get superstitious about it
until a carload of us went with him
on the anniversary of that boy's death
and watched it dive on the windshield
and then veer full-force into the fence
to crucify itself in the two top strands
and leave us with a heartsick feeling
like that boy had died all over again.

The dead crow graced that fence for months
lapped somehow in those two strands
its spread wings shining as stark reminders
of bewilderments better left unmentioned
and sentiments that carried him farther back
to brief boyhood games of chance and chase
belonging to an almost forgotten world.
When it had sufficiently dried and withered
and the ants had done their quiet work
and a white bone or two peeped through
the fading luminance in the black feathers
he finally took it down and buried it
but left those strands in their tangle
for time or the weather to separate
though he still remembers the exact spot
and still goes out there to tag in.

Whiling Time

It tricks you in the end, time does!
Your mind's eye wanders off
to inherit something almost magical
and you end up sick and squandered
or so say old unscrubbed men
balanced on the bottle crates
espousing their gas station philosophy
while digging out shards of grime
from under hard thick talons
with the worn-down blade of a Barlow.

In the end it gets you, something does!
Pray to God it will be quick
and spare you undue suffering
or wetting all over yourself
says one who has to stretch himself
while two of them push bottle caps
across the ragged checkered squares
and squint at each passing car
mumbling all kinds of "sonsofbitches"
if the tag is from out of state.

Leave a Message

This is Cecil
I figure we could meet at the Speedway
and go early enough in the afternoon
to get those seats by the pit entrance
and be all set for the stock car race.
If you'll get Maylene to make potato salad
I'll bring an ice chest full of sweet drinks
and we'll buy the hotdogs at the concession
to keep from having to tote so much.
If that Elrod boy is racing tonight
we're liable to see a five car pileup.
He ain't nothing but a rubber-burning fool
ran that Breedlove boy right into the stands
over at the fairgrounds track last December
killed him and two more deader'n a wedge
one wudn't no more'n six years old.
I saw him all mashed to a pulp
and his mama wringing hands and screamin'
that's why I want to get there early
and get them high seats over the pit
safest place for women and children to be.
With Junior Elrod hot and out for blood
there's sure to be a bad wreck or two.
Buzz me back when you get off
and we'll figure out how many's going
otherwise I'll just meet you out there.
Ten-four!

This is Cecil again
Mabel just walked in and told me
about the layoffs out at the shirt plant
said they might spread down to Mixon's
and that you've been puttin' some feelers out
and you're looking at that post office job
they're interviewing for over at Brysonville.

Now I ain't one to direct your traffic
but I'm here to tell you straight out
it's dangerous working for the public
especially in one of those government jobs.
Hell, some crazy ass working there for years
can all of a sudden have a bad day
and start blowing good people away.
It don't matter to him who gets shot.
It's just a mindless, random act
with you staring down the barrel.
It wouldn't hurt you to mull that one over.
A lotta people laugh and say I'm paranoid
but I'm going to tell you like it is
just 'cause you're paranoid don't mean
that somebody ain't out to get you.
Call me back if you make it in
and don't forget about the potato salad.
I'll see you out there at the pit.
Yeah, buddy!

Days of Brass

At the end of all we are
when what has been compiled
no longer suits prevailing sentiments
and transient memories floating by
are neither precious nor unkind
mind well that when we walked
this green and yearning earth
and felt it yield beneath our shoes
like so many loves fed and flown
we knew the power of flesh
the taste of salt on skin
the heat in looks that lay
like haze on days of brass.

After the last quiet disowning
of all that has turned and fled
after deep and silent loathing
for the remnants that escaped
time in its patient doing
would have you stand fast
and mark how we are made
to sit by the hills we climbed
with a sorrow in our hearts
or mill in humble penitence
like geese wandering in a yard
or move about like wraiths
untouched and unlamented.

Safe Haven

As a winter night closed in
just past the laying of the wind
promising a rime of morning frost
on three souls up near Red Mountain
setting about to search for wood
they came upon an oak long dead
and long devoid of limb or leaf
seasoned to its hollow core
with all the instant prospects
of a fast and roaring fire.

It broke open when it fell
with width enough to get cold fingers
into the musk of jagged cracks
to pry open its dark heart
but spring enough to hold intact
the grisly remnants of an occupant
who wedged there years before
and had tried to scrape and claw
and cut his way back out
with a broken-bladed pocket knife.

Those who built their modest fire
and talked well into the night
beside this gleaming companion
found by the next day's light
inscriptions carved into the wood
just above the rack of bones

and surmised from faint lettering
that he had fled from Indians
to the protection of the tree
and had hidden all too well.

Safe Haven: A periodical entitled, *Grave Matters* (v3, n3, Aug. 1997) described this story taken from *Weekly Iron Age*, Tallapoosa County, Alabama, 2-12-1855. The body discovered in the hollow tree was identified as that of B.B. Turner, the name inscribed on the bone handle pocket knife. The carved words were, "I fell," and "hiding," and "Ind. ." The article cites that the three men retained the skull of the skeleton and the piece of wood containing the message.

Over the Wall

Go figure
and when you do
count the guard's paces
each day and night
until you know by heart
the moments of abandonment
when only God sees
and train yourself to skirt
the oval of the searchlight
so that it never falls
like iron on one
incriminating piece of you.

When all has been done
to memorize the moves
and calibrate the odds
that improve or lessen
all risks or chances
it will then be time
to swallow one's heart
and pull embedded feet
from their weighted places
like uprooting plants
and wither with the fright
of going over the wall.

A Death in the Woods

With a pearl mist lifting off the bottoms
and gray air sprites bathing everything
trapped by their floating beads
he field-stripped a last limp cigarette
and dropped it on the fresh macadam road
barely able to squint and make out
the bobbing tail of an English setter
moving like a silent metronome
and sifting through rank wringing grasses
bird working the sallow fields.

Easing out into the wet morass
once covert thoughts and schemes stopped
and the dog reached and held a rigid point
his finger touched the damp safety
of the light-weight .20-gauge Franchi
cradled close and loaded with No. 7s
and his heart quickened yet dreaded
the inevitability of this dark ritual
drawing him into its violent eye
as if he had no choice.

Halfway through the waist-high sea
pulling against him like dragnets
he circled wide and far away
to sit for a time in the woods
and plumb the depths of true desires
with the dog still statuesque and trembling
and knowing it was apt to ruin her
came back behind her arrowed stance
so as not to disturb the covey
and whispered, "Come on, girl! Let's go!"

Signature

The child in us can go
all the way there and back
without tripping on stairs
lying loose-boarded and uneven
or being lost in the dark
that waits behind all doors
to old beckoning cellars.

Such a starred and fated child
will not be scarred or singed
or harmed or hampered
in this rush of what has been
through all the turns and twists
and sighs of years unraveling
like a worn string ball

But will always live to bear
the great inner wrenchings
that crush like leaden weights
with all the levity of light
shining from a diamond eye
and be bidden from the source
to go blithely, blithely.

Fit To Kill

Nobody paid attention to Lurlene
until that night she went to church
all decked out and slinking in a dress
that fit her body like a wetsuit
revealing more than anyone had seen
or could imagine on the dullest evening
under lights dimmed soft and low
at the Peavine Baptist prayer meeting.

When it came her turn to kneel
in a gathering aura of her own perfume
every righteous eye was wide open
focused on her black spiked heels
or the rounded seam running its wickedness
up the back side of her net mesh hose
like a main road on a travel map
that went right to the county seat.

Ruth Allgood punched her husband Pleas
to take his eyes off those shapely legs
just as Lit Simmons dropped a hymnal
that landed directly on the sore corn
of his wife Wilma's right little toe
causing her to stand straight up
and let out a loud, "God bless it!"
that shocked the docile back to life.

All through the text and evening message
the preacher stammered like a child
trying hard not to gawk or stare

at the sultry figure sitting right up front
as he preached on the woman Jezebel
finally ending when his failing voice
broke into a high falsetto note
like a dog put out of its misery.

It took an instant for the last amen
to work its will into the quick
of all but the lagging and reluctant
who, once outside, between quick puffs
asked each other the timeless question:
"Wonder what got into Lurlene?"
And one old saint among them said,
"Some women just take notions!"

Night Beat

Old ghosts need their sleep
but there are some on stakeout
who still work the graveyard shift
years past the evil that we did.
They cannot desist or let go
of deceptions, sins or slights
no longer applicable to us
but show their pure contempt
in how they dog our every step
or keep surveillance as we sleep
and we who suffer badly from
distastefulness we may have caused
or the humiliations and rejections
lying squarely at our door
cannot assuage them with remorse
or interest them in a confession.
All we can do is lie here
and wait for the shift to change
hoping they will be replaced
by those naive and more inclined
to show us heartfelt sympathy
when we rise and face ourselves.

Crop Duster

He got all the way there and back
without so much as a scratch
and he had flown and fought his way
from jungles to hilltop reaches
of the China-Burma-India theater
first in a worn-out Curtiss Hawk
that coughed and clawed its way skyward
clearing its throat and spitting black plumes
before kissing the backside of the thirties
and then in streamlined P-51's
fresh from the Los Angeles assembly line
that pushed their way right through
the myths of an invincible empire
to claim a larger wedge of sky.

He'd pinned the wings and campaign ribbons
to the seat strap of his Beech Staggerwing
and worn them every time he'd flown
rising ghost-like from the grassy strip
to swoop down over quiet cotton fields
with the fiery mien of yesteryear
and spray them with the same precision
with which he strafed advancing Japanese
and then climb upward in an arc
to gain the larger wholesale view
owning, if just for a little while,
the flood of hard-bought exhilaration
that fills the soul with triumph
before coming back down to land.

A Brief Noel

Nothing warms and heals so much
as Christmas lights seen from the road
shining in the night's great emptiness
with their shafts of red and green
their multicolored auras streaming
from the haft of a deep and friendless void
and then spilling out into the eyes
of the pressed and rushed and misdirected
softening all pinched looks of despair
all remembered griefs, all old regrets
all fearful thoughts and intuitions
that ride grim and uninvited
like skeletal passengers in the car
trapping in the senses with one glance
in the brief-lit, rear view mirror
the tastes and smells of ancient finds
the clear notes of lost carols sung
in sparkling cold outside a windowed tree
the white breaths of children gathered
at a makeshift crib to see a doll
that always had its upraised arms
frozen in a sign of peace.

At the Submarine Museum

Looking in the display cases
the names and stories come alive
as one is spirited back to the Pacific
and to the deck of the *Growler*
on that rain-soaked February night
when Gilmore ordered her to dive
knowing if she did, he'd drown . . .
or to the bowels of the *Seawolf*
plunging like a lead weight
nine thousand, six hundred feet
and taking her crew down with her
to the murk of the ocean floor
where she died from lack of air
without ever knowing why.

Reading the wall of ships' plaques
cannot do justice to the iron resolve
or educate one to the courage
behind the hard jaw of Mush Morton
guiding a stricken *Wahoo*
through the bristling Perouse Strait
tempting fate and leaking oil
unable to avoid the last ashcan
that cracked her like a walnut . . .
or the pluck of Cromwell on *Sculpin*
staring down the barrels of a destroyer
and making the irrevocable choice
to go down with the ship
rather than risk enemy capture.

Youngsters come to gawk
and look through the periscope
but have never felt on their faces
the telling beads of icy fear

that dripped from chin to deck
while sighting through the lens
like McKenzie on the *Triton*
or Bole on board the *Amberjack*
trading lives and boats for time
in the swelter of the Solomons
and stemming the tide of Japanese
in their transports and munition ships
on their way to war and mayhem
unchecked but for these silent few.

One can still tour the rusting hulks
of some who made it home
the *Batfish* aging in Muskogee
or *Silversides* asleep in Muskegon
and the *Bowfin, Drum* and *Croaker*
in their respective mothball parks
but the rest are remembered here
with old photographs and citations
that call their names and feats to mind
and with murmured prayers still lifted
for the ones so quickly cut into scrap
or sealed and strung like bobbing corks
and for the many who are out there
still on patrol.

At the Submarine Museum: The museum is located in the coastal town of St. Marys, Georgia. Nearby is the submarine support base at Kings Bay. The museum reflects World War II displays as well as those of more current submarine history. Fifty-two United States submarines were lost during World War II.

Best Way

Most old counsel would not apply
unless a world still turned
that fed fried rabbit for breakfast
and that still used half dollars
as weights to hold down the lids
of a dead man's eyes.

The mentoring is long outdated
that canonized who owned what farm
on after-dinner Sunday rides
or that refought the bloody battles
on late whippoorwill evenings
with branch kin on the porch.

Pushing cars to jump them off
or knowing where to find fat lighter
or how to hone a dull knife blade
serve as the vestiges of times taken
and are as useless to the modern life
as planting by the phases of the moon.

But if one is to be preserved
and hallowed far beyond what those
who spurn the past might think
then let it stand that the best way
to eat a tomato sandwich is
with sleeves rolled up over a sink.

Grave Matters

Dogs howled like they were scalded
the night old man Dewey Renfroe died
letting off such a God-awful racket
somebody had to go under the porch
and jerk them out by the hindquarters
getting that odor all over their hands
and sneezing from the dust kicked up
in disrupting all those little bug drills.

They had to sell off his hogs
and what few scrub cows he kept
leaving just that old white mule
after the wife killed the yard chickens.
Tom Burkhalter took it home with him
just to get shed of it for her
and it laid down and died on him
but that ain't the funny thing.

The wife left a silk arrangement
at the head of Dewey's new grave
to brighten the barren spot a little
and take her mind off those clods
just heaped high and left there
then went back the next afternoon
to find it moved two lots over
to the grave of Sue Mae Kilcrease.

It really got off with the wife
as she was Sue Mae's rival once
back in Dewey's early sparkin' days
and she figured like the rest of us
on it being the work of Dell Ray

that'd be Sue Mae's only child
who either stays shut up at home
or is out walking in the cemetery.

She got a mean lick on the head
not long after she went to crawling
crawled right off the porch, I think
and was never the same after that;
never learned who her daddy was
as far as the rest of us know
but always took a shine to Dewey
till her Mama scolded her about it.

As to who took them silk flowers
if it wasn't Dell Ray's hand in it
we'd be hard put to place the blame.
Friends told the wife to forget about it
on account of Dell Ray being retarded
but folks like her got a heap of sense
especially when it comes right down
to knowing which buttons to push.

Fire

If fire were such that it could come
subdued enough and safe enough
for one to stay just ahead of it
snatching up all of the precious things
old joys might be spared the worst
and old sorrows simply left to burn
but with fire being what it is
without restraints to check or guide
there is no time to ferret through
the residue of lives and years
as they are ravaged and consumed
no time to halt or stem or slow
this insatiable will to reduce us
once again to dust and ashes.

Walking Death

The town doctor could not reach it
so Uncle Bob went back to his spot
on the bench by the water oak
fronting Snelson's corner store
for the fifth day with a fish bone
lodged crossways in his throat
and with a look pale and fearful
of a man about to die.

To swallow meant to strangle
so breaths were short and shallow
as he wiped saliva at the corners
to keep the coughing fits at bay
unable to speak above a whisper
lest dreaded spasms act with force
to drive the jagged barb in deeper
and doom all hope of its release.

On that warm November afternoon
as ancient eyes caught white seeds
adrift on the breeze and blowing by
bearing dreams soft-spun and weightless
he watched them lift above his head
wondering if flown spirits rose on air
and if his own would find its way
to a home in the fields of God.

The talk inside the store ranged
from: "Sure is bad about Uncle Bob"
to: "He's just a case of walking death"
as children were reminded one by one
to give the sufferer a wide berth
and friends spoke soft encouragements
or simply stayed inside the store
to spare themselves the fright.

Then Rilla come in for her snuff
and after taking a mighty dip
which packed and puffed her bottom lip
set out to cure this helplessness
with wadded balls of white bread
pressed from the fresh-made slices
convincing Uncle Bob to chew them
into one large and solid lump.

"When you force it down," she said
"There won't be no comin' back!
Hit's gonna break that bone loose
or you gonna die and be with God
and I'll be right here to hold you."
No hope shone from that wrinkled face
as tears ran down new-made gutters
and hands gripped black on white.

With one last and longing look at the sky
he closed his eyes and swallowed hard
as customers stood by slack-jawed
half expecting him to keel right over
yet cheated out of this premonition
when he broke loose, then stood up,
smiled and hugged the life from Rilla
body wracking with great iron sobs.

Having been silenced for many days
all were confident of his first words
being recitations of profound gratitude
and were amazed to hear him say
with great calmness and conviction:
"I caught that fish using dough-balls
but I'd never have believed that one
could snag it for the second time."

Herman's Thumb

It was a bitter chill unnoticed
in its record-breaking downward plunge
with the mercury huddled in a silver ball
and the wind knifing its vengeance
through the gristle of the land
yet Herman came to work his will
upon the dried hay in darkened barns
rousing stock to feed and milk
then hitching horses as they balked
and jerked their chains the instant
his thumb was in a rusted link.

It was a bitter wound unnoticed
stamping around in numbing blackness
mindful only of life's little chores
done with dull and transient thought
while blowing white frost in billows
prior to a hard breaking of the day
yet once inside the lighted house
surprised to see the purple stump
he pined but birthed the adage
used only when a winter morning
is as cold as Herman's thumb.

Homemade Sin

The recurring dream first took her breath
the night her older sister died
cancer-riddled in her seventieth year
with sunken flesh and fragile form
pressed down so far into the casket
she no longer resembled the pretty girl
with skin as smooth as river rocks
standing beside the "Join the Navy" poster
in a forties drugstore window.

The dream harkened back to that time
and the dirt lane out in the country
leading from the house to the road
where the dreamer as a child would walk
past yellow bell and quince and plum
to the mailbox on the fence post
and pull down the rusted metal lid
and reach into its deep black throat
to find a coiled and hissing snake inside.

It came back every night for months
to exact its harsh, sweat-soaked tribute
until she saw someone about it
unraveling the hem of her childhood
as he sat behind a polished desk
observing her through black-rimmed lenses
and listening as she dredged the bottom
in seven hourlong, post-hypnotic sessions
and snagged the tale within the tale.

Up it came to the shining surface
cresting like a bloated body set free
from the dark, subconscious undertow

as she remembered reaching in the box
with trembling hand and jealous heart
to intercept her older sister's letters
from the sailor who sent his love
which she would read and rip in half
and then pretend they never came.

His submarine was lost with all hands
going down in waters as dark and gray-green
as a pane of window glass seen end-on
dragging the memory of her guilt with it
to lie entombed in silt and silence
until a yellow lightning flash of insight
released enough of its grisly flotsam
for her to cry out and confess
that she was the snake in the mailbox.

Such knowledge cannot be forever borne
in the long and tedious night watches
or carried with the burdens of each day
and that is why it was relinquished
on a warm and moonlit night thereafter
when she went down to the millpond
with inner power and a great resolve
to jump in and go to her sister
bare-souled to beg her forgiveness.

Behind the Door

Behind the door
a promised spring awaits
though on this side of it
as swift as late-night horsemen
roam the unforgiving phantoms
of fear and death and war
marrying us to their rituals
owning us in our darkness
teaching us that life is random
and hope delusional.

Do not forget that we are here
in place of countless others
swimming the same sea
and that to us is given
the crispness of this moment
the graciousness of this time
in aromatic bursts of mornings
and the silks of peaceful nights
while all else the heart requires
lies just behind the door.

End of the Line

Out where the rails have rusted
and spider legs of Bermuda
have crept like cemetery grass
between gray and withered crossties
he languishes in the wheelchair
fumbling with a pocket watch
and adjusting the greasy bill
of an old striped railroad cap
as he squints at a bright spot
off to the west.

His daughter brings him here
in the county's senior van
and lets him gently down
on the new hydraulic lift
to sit for a good hour
with the smell of diesel
strong in his senses
though not a trace of it
has been upon these tracks
for over thirty years.

Here where the tall weeds
hum with the stir of crickets
and a slight touch of fall
is felt down to the marrow
he reminisces the old days
when he rode the *Crescent*
at top speed and full throttle
across this lonesome stretch
like a great silver blur
outrunning the starlit dawn.

Not far from this spot
he'd watched a lithe figure
silhouetted in the high beam
motion for the horn to blow
on a year of midnight runs
and farther up the line
midway of the one hard bend
he'd seen a man rise up
from the shadows of the track
and could not stop in time.

The scene has been with him
since the night it happened
and he sometimes sees himself
taking that man's place
rising in the prime of life
to meet the train head-on.
Sometimes he swears it's better
than being here like this
not knowing what's waiting
at the end of the line.

In Essence

Morning shone from the brown bottle
when she bought the vanilla extract
from the tailgate of a Watkins truck
and held its dark amber to the sun
never having heard of Xanath
or the eccentricities of her passion
but mimicking her story perfectly
in how she baked a pound cake
adding more precious drops of it
than the yellowed recipe required.

When she took the offering to him
warm and golden from the oven
and wrapped in a red checkered cloth
the aroma of that extra flavoring
gave off its nostalgic perfume
as eyes met and hearts touched
and the old rooster-head clicked once
then struck its fury on the hour
snatching them back to time and place
and from hopes that were not to be.

The stroke had drawn him to one side
like fire withering a flowering plant
taking his speech at sixty-four
and curling fingers on one hand
subjecting him all the more completely
to the oversight of an aged mother
who hovered and withdrew in turn
broach fastened to a sunken throat
and cold eyes glittering like ice
impatient for his visitor to leave.

They had waited out the long years
of her iron rule and stern demeanor
thinking to outlive her beating heart
and have some prospects for a life
only to be shown a glimpse of it
down to its hard and bitter ending
as she placed the cake beside him
fully aware that such soft goodness
soaked in its own familiar smell
was all that she could give him now.

In Essence: In Totonac legend, a goddess named Xanath fell in love with an earthly warrior. They were prevented from a life together because she could not become human, and he could not be made immortal. Xanath could neither marry the warrior nor abandon him, so she changed herself into the vanilla orchid and became the sacred plant which gave the warrior and his people her eternal presence. See: Bonnie Busenberg. *Vanilla, Chocolate & Strawberry: The Story of Your Favorite Flavors.* Lerner Publications. 1994. p. 17.

Postscript

If I were to unroll a rug and chant
my contemplations from a rooftop
when the east grows pink then orange
my prayer of the day would be for you
its words taking flight on a dove's wing
that when you have wandered in darkness
love might find you and bring you back
that on the rare day of blessing
when you splash in the streams of joy
all your hopes might be pure
that as you look in the eyes of age
you may behold the heart of a child
and that the last day like the first
will be fresh with wonder.